VEGETABLE CAKES

VEGETABLE CAKES

The most fun way to five a day!

YSANNE SPEVACK

photographs by Nicki Dowey

LORENZ BOOKS

Contents

Vegetable Cakes!

Why aren't we using vegetables in dessert? That seems obvious – they're not as sweet as fruit. Until you think more and realise that a lot of fruits are quite tart to taste, and many veggies are quite sweet. We all know there's a spectrum – every child will tell you that many vegetables are really fruits, including avocados, tomatoes, peas, sweet corn, courgettes, and bell peppers. In fact, so many vegetables are technically fruits, this book could almost be called 'Fruit cakes', or 'Cakes made with fruits that aren't as popular as apples and pears'!

I've made sure however to include not only veggies that are secretly fruits, but also ones that are 100% bona-fide vegetables, such as carrots, lettuce, spinach, cauliflower and onions. Why conform to the norm, let's embrace the strange, and say yes to vegetables in unusual places! Vegetables are delicious, and they can all be sweetened, either by being marinated and mixed with something sweet (and healthy), or by having their natural sugars caramelised – or both.

Many vegetables offer us other plus points, like outrageous colours, or surprising textures. Take beetroots – how could you turn down such a wonderful colour? And lotus roots – the crunch and the shape are too extraordinary to refuse. The gorgeous spiralling shapes of the fiddlehead ferns make a tart of true artistry.

And, of course, there are the health benefits of eating more veg. Many people struggle with ways to eat their recommended five (or more) a day, and parents often worry about getting vegetables into their children without a fight. Children are savvy to every trick to smuggle veg into their dinner, and can find the evidence of a speck of green in a veggie burger within seconds. But, give them a cake with a big cauliflower inside, and the silliness of it gets a foot in the door. The pure anarchy of putting soft leaves inside a layer cake or loaf engages most people's sense of humour. Once you're there, Godzilla Cake (page 40) is a cinch! Other ideas are things of pure beauty, whether cascading radish slices offering unexpected juicy crispness to a pavlova, or swirls of purple radicchio adorning a rich and creamy cheesecake.

Widen your perspective and enter into a brave new parallel world of possibilities. These recipes may feature some of the most familiar ingredients in your fridge, but in an enlightening and often entertaining way. Lastly, but most importantly of all, the cakes, bakes, cookies and treats that follow are all absolutely wonderful to eat – which is our aim, to indulge in the pleasures of baking and eating, with a side helping of health along the way.

Enjoying Vegetables in Cakes and Desserts

Eat more vegetables – that's a simple aim for people everywhere. It's the one thing that unites all healthy eating philosophies – vegetables. There's not a single diet that doesn't encourage you to enjoy more veg.

But, vegetables don't need to be limited to the savoury course. Why stick to vegetables as sides, or salads? These wonderful fresh ingredients have so much more potential. So here's how we can expand our repertoire, be more creative in the kitchen, and eat more vegetables: by including them in cakes!

At first, it sounds unappetising, until we remember that we've always loved carrot cake. In America, zucchini bread is a classic dessert – and then there's pumpkin pie, as pervasive as apple pie. Including vegetables in dessert recipes and bakes is not new, but we can feature more varieties of vegetables in more varied ways, and making sure they are used in higher quantities, to sing at the heart of each recipe.

In this baking book with a difference, I've featured new ideas and revisited some of the classics too, by adding flavours and twists so that a new generation can enjoy the traditional ideas, but with a fresh and interesting spin. I've also paid attention to other ways we want to look after ourselves, by making sure every recipe isn't too sweet, and doesn't include the kinds of ingredients we're keen to avoid. And I've delighted in using more of the pleasurable things in life like culinary flowers and herbs.

We aim to eat less refined sugar, good flours, less dairy or animal-derived ingredients, and less processed ingredients, whatever their origins. We prefer organic, locally grown and seasonal ingredients where possible. Some of these recipes are paleo-friendly, and many of them are also raw and vegan. Others include butter and eggs and honey, and were developed with busy parents in mind. Armed with this book, you'll be able to smuggle a few more veggies into your children's meals – as a cake! And in wonderful cookies, muffins, tarts, and cheesecakes...

Many of these recipes are brazen about the vegetables they contain. For example, Maple Lemon Veggie Slab Pie, which courageously contains bell peppers, celeriac and

Left and right: some familiar-looking cakes and some rather more surprising ones – the chocolate coconut cream layer looks temptingly traditional, as do the cupcakes, slab pie and traybake, albeit with unexpected decoration – but those brave enough to try the salady pie will be thrilled to find it tastes of salted caramel!

butternut squash alongside the maple syrup and lemons. Or Mizuna Macaroons, which bizarrely request you whip up the cooking water from a can of chickpeas before adding large quantities of puréed mizuna leaves.

I'm fully aware of how eccentric some of these recipes sound, but this is the thing – they work! If you're looking for new ideas that taste delicious, that satisfy your need to include more vegetables in your diet, and which allow you to indulge in all the fun of sweet baking, this cookbook is for you.

Using and Choosing Vegetables

At first glance, fruits are the most obvious fresh produce to include in desserts, because they have a higher natural sugar content than vegetables. It's true, fruits are sweeter than vegetables, on the whole. But on closer examination, this isn't always the case. If you taste a particularly tart apple or a sharp strawberry alongside a caramelised bite of butternut squash or even a well-roasted onion, you'll agree that vegetables can definitely be sweeter than fruit, without adding any sweetener.

Let's focus instead on flavours. Is there any reason that the delicate herbal flavour of parsnips can't be enjoyed in cake? Or how about fennel – you could enjoy the aniseed notes in fennel while sinking your teeth into a creamy cheesecake. And what about artichokes – imagine that special tangy but buttery flavour inside a delicate little cake instead of always wrapped up with salt and vinegar.

This book will guide you deep into the land of vegetable cakes, cookies, and even cheesecakes. You'll find wild vegetables like fiddlehead ferns cooked into pretty galettes, and nettles that feature in crisp almond biscotti that are the perfect with a cup of hot nettle tea.

Of course, flavours and nutrients are intrinsically linked. The flavours in fresh produce are tiny microchemicals that are simultaneously good for you – we've evolved to find them pleasurable; it's our bodies' ingenious way of guiding us to eat the healthiest things for us.

Vegetables can be used fresh for preference, or frozen (frozen peas are absolutely sweet and easy to use, as any child will tell you). In fact frozen vegetables often contain more nutrients than fresh ones, although that can seem counter-intuitive – freezing very freshly-picked veggies keeps the heat and light-sensitive nutrients intact, although there can also be a loss in texture. Canned vegetables, on the other hand, are always lower in nutrients, as the canning process involves a lot of heat, which is one of the main things that destroy nutrients, along with light and exposure to air. I do occasionally buy canned palm hearts or canned artichoke hearts, more as a flavouring for quick winter salads than a central ingredient. But they do have the benefit of being very soft and I often use them in the velvety little muffin-type cakes on page 78.

The only other canned vegetables I use regularly are beans – not sliced green beans, but pulses. They offer exceptional benefits in terms of convenience, and the high-pressure nature of the canning process produces beautifully soft textures in the finished product. I always keep a can of black beans for this reason and also, a can of chickpeas and white beans. The reason I use canned chickpeas and white beans is twofold – firstly, because that means very quick and softly-textured hummus in moments (that's another book!), but increasingly because of the bean water, which can be used as an egg-replacement in many recipes. Simply whip the drained fibre-rich liquid from the can of chickpeas or white beans, and it will turn into something that looks like whipped egg whites in a matter of minutes. Check out the recipes for pavlova on page 26, pancakes on page 44, and macarons on page 128 (and others) to find out more.

In general, however, I do recommend using fresh vegetables. Three elements need to be avoided to extend the life of fresh produce: heat, light and air. Fresh vegetables are best in terms of flavour, but they need to be eaten quickly. Leaf vegetables like lettuces and spinach lose half of their nutrients within a week of being picked if they're stored in a plastic bag in the fridge. Vitamin C, thiamin and folic acid are very unstable after a vegetable or fruit has been picked, so 50% is likely to be lost after a few days, even if refrigerated perfectly. The best way to store fresh vegetables is in a bag that's perforated with little holes that allow carbon dioxide to naturally leave the produce. Keep the veg under wraps in the crisper drawer of the fridge, where there's more humidity. The exception are potatoes, which are best stored in a cupboard. For fresh herbs and flowers, keep

Right and left: many vegetables are as naturally sweet and as gorgeously coloured as fruits, which you can use to full advantage in cakes (and other treats).

them in a glass of water in the fridge door, covered with a plastic or wax paper bag. They will last much longer that way, and stay plump and hydrated. Mushrooms need to be stored in paper bags, not plastic, and eaten quickly before they dry out. If they do dry out, of course, they can still be used by reconstituting, as with any dried mushrooms.

For all fresh produce, remember that they can easily be made to look fresher and more nutritious than they really are. The reason that produce from a farmers' market invariably spoils quicker than the same varieties in a supermarket is down to technology. Shelf-life extension techniques like irradiation, and modified atmosphere packaging (i.e. bagged greens), are useful for cutting down waste and adding convenience, but the extension of beauty and the aesthetic of freshness doesn't equate to the real nutritional content of the food. The lettuce from the farmers' market that looks soggy and inedible after a week may have the same nutritional value as the lettuce from the supermarket that looks crisp and usable after the same period of time. The varieties also make a huge difference. Rocket or arugula is not in fact in the lettuce family – it's a special type of wild cabbage. That's why it's far more nutritious to start with, than something like iceberg lettuce.

As a general rule, buying vegetables in small batches and eating them when they're fresh is definitely the best way to go. And if that's not realistic for your household schedule, frozen veggies are a great option to have as a kitchen backup.

Roots and Tubers

I'm going to start with beetroots. The colour, the colour... how are these sweet, darkly-flavoured balls of deepness not more widely enjoyed at teatime? And they partner with chocolate like Dr. Watson partners with Sherlock Holmes. Don't shy away from the raw or the cooked varieties – both have a place.

Next carrots, the most widely enjoyed vegetable in cakes, probably because they're sweet! Purée steamed carrots for an instant sweet compote, or roast them with cinnamon for a classic dessert, perhaps with a drizzle of orange blossom flower water and honey, and then sprinkled with ground coriander and cinnamon. Add a scoop of ice-cream and a simple biscuit for the ultimate

Top left: beetroots are two vegetables in one, with their roots and tops, and the visually stunning lotus root is as good in sweet as it is in savoury bakes. Golden corn, emerald peas and ruby radishes offer a cookery jewel box.

mid-week instant dessert that's also elegant enough to serve at a party. Don't hold back from trying out the different heirloom varieties of carrot, found in the prettiest shades from purple to white.

Celeriac is a particularly ugly vegetable, and as such, it's an obvious choice for the food processor. Chop it into tiny rice-sized bits and use it as a flour replacement in some recipes, or cut into slivers or cubes and tuck into a tart. Celeriac is an unloved member of the carrot family, but offers notes of angelica and wild fennel if you let them out by adding a little fennel pollen and wildflower honey. Don't allow petty prejudice to get in the way of this delicately flavoured vegetable becoming a beloved member of your repertoire.

On the other end of the beauty spectrum are lotus roots, so pretty! The delicate chestnut-like flavour works wonderfully in sweet recipes. Then, there are parsnips. Chances are, roasted caramelised parsnips are on your list of nostalgic dishes. We love their sticky sweetness, and the promise of the occasional crispy bit if they've been over-cooked. Well, the natural progression of this line of thinking is my Parsnip Upside Down Tarte on page 104, which is modelled on an apple tart tatin.

Radishes are a little more challenging in terms of bite and lack of sweetness, but their texture and aesthetic encourage experimentation. Radishes are a garnish staple, and beg for an updated spin on the traditional 1950s-style roses. If they're soaked in water, they do all sorts of fun things, and if the water is sweetened and flavoured, these same properties can be harnessed for dessert – you can do this with the glorious pavlova on page 26.

Sunchokes are tubers that are related to sunflowers, hence the name. They have a similar flavour to sunflower seeds for this reason, and a wonderful delicate texture. They're also known as Jerusalem artichokes, or earth apples. Whatever you call them, they contain inulin, which is a natural carbohydrate that's similar to fructose, and is why they have a natural sweetness, as well as the tendency to be tricky to digest for some. Yacon is another tuber that contains a lot of inulin, and it's often used dried as a mild caramel-tasting sweetener.

Potatoes aren't an obvious choice for dessert recipes, unless you start to include potato flour, in which case, they're fairly ubiquitous in gluten-free baking. Mashed potatoes are very useful as a creamy base for all kinds of sweet flavours, and they're fantastic when coarsely grated and fried, not unlike pakora or latkes, but transformed with a sweet syrup or combined with other grated ingredients, such as sweet potatoes. Sweet potatoes aren't related to potatoes, nor are the similar yam (which is the name by which they are often known in the States), but their sweet, sticky properties do make them ideal for many dessert recipes, from mousses to cakes.

Swedes take some thought, with their radish-like bite, but once cooked they have a lovely consistency and colour that can absolutely work in dessert recipes, and the crunch fades. It's the same with turnips, which have the additional benefit of coming in such pretty colours. Shave thin slivers of turnips of every colour, soak in flower waters, and use them to decorate the sweet of your choice.

VEGETABLE FRUITS

A somewhat problematic vegetable fruit in savoury cuisine, the red, yellow and purple bell pepper sings in sweets. Char their skins and blacken their hearts to elicit their sweetest notes. And always drench them in oils, whether that's butter or another kind of fat; I recommend playing with nut or seed oils. Also, we should mention chilli peppers, as they're a classic with anything chocolate. Less obvious is okra. When we think about okra, we usually consider its texture first; the little pods that are also known as ladies' fingers aren't the go-to ingredient for a cake. But, if it's moisture retention you're looking for, okra deliver in spades and is the reason why the Okra Cacao Bundt Cake recipe on page 38 isn't silly at all but deliciously moist and destined to become a favourite.

Finally, as every child knows, the tomato is really a fruit. Here, we get to treat them as such. Many of the tomato-based recipes you've made could have been sweet instead of savoury if you'd omitted the onions, garlic and salt, and instead added a spoonful of honey. Just try the Tomato and Almond Cake on page 42. I do prefer cherry tomatoes for most things, though make an exception when I find big heirloom tomato varieties at the height of their ripeness and fresh from the garden or farmers' market. Also, it is worth noting that chocolate-coloured tomato varieties are sweeter than the red ones, and therefore chocolate cherry tomatoes hit the jackpot.

BRASSICAS

As with many of the cruciferous vegetables, broccoli isn't an obvious dessert ingredient. That said, it's a flower, so what could be prettier than bringing out the beauty of the florets? Soak in honey or maple syrup, and suddenly the sulphurous tones wane, and the natural sweetness blossoms. Another way to sweeten anything is to apply heat – roasting something even as sulphur-y as Brussels sprouts works well. Try basting cauliflower, Brussels or broccoli in lashings of coconut oil sprinkled with

Left and below: bell peppers and fennel are sweet and easy to use, especially when caramelised. Okra is moist and delicate, and amazingly compatible with chocolate!

Above: cauliflowers, broccoli, Romanesco and Brussels sprouts are flowers and buds, and become much more obvious as potential cake ingredients when viewed as such. The sweetness of butternut squash has long been utilised in cakes of course, but now takes centre stage.

coconut sugar, cinnamon and warmly-flavoured ground cardamom. Heavenly.

Cauliflower is the standout ingredient for paleo people, and a ridiculously handy vegetable for baking enthusiasts, whatever their relationship with nuts and grains. Step One – chop it into breadcrumb-sized bits, using a grater or a food processor. Step Two – tip it into a clean cloth, and squeeze out the juice into a bowl for use in something else, for example, a soup. Step Three – voila, you have a new kind of ingredient that's not chopped nuts, and not flour, but is somewhere between the two. It's ready to be baked into cookies and cakes, and makes a mean cheesecake base. In this book we have the cauliflower layer cake on page 30 and cauli cupcakes on page 68, among others. There are also Romanesco cauliflowers – I welcome the beauty of these at any course, savoury or sweet, just check out the Godzilla Cake on page 40.

Onto cabbage; I love green but favour purple for many recipes. They taste almost identical, but the colour! Red (and blue and purple) cabbage is a time-honoured natural dye for everything from cheeses to textiles, and there's no reason we can't continue to be inspired by its vibrant

spectrum of hues. Boiling destroys cabbage's ability to dye other ingredients red or blue, but does stabilise its claims to purple. Also you can always make a paste with it in a food processer and blend this paste to bring purple hues to something white, like dried coconut.

And now to kale. This trendy vegetable is not the sweetest vegetable and its texture isn't the softest. A confession, kale, I love you in salad, and you're fantastic in most savoury things, but you aren't always my first vegetable choice for desserts. Nonetheless I've successfully smuggled you into my Kale Matcha Cookies recipe on page 124, and you are the undeniable star of the cake on page 24.

Squashes

Pumpkin. An oldie, but a goodie. Pie, yes, and also muffins and cookies. It's also widely enjoyed as a dessert ingredient in Asia, often as a mousse, or as a filling for rice-based pastries. Butternut squashes are a natural for desserts – just bake and mash, and it's already a sweet pie filling. Add Christmas spices and yogurt, and it's an instant syllabub. I think butternut is even better than pumpkin in pumpkin pie, and they're an inexpensive, easy entry-vegetable for cooks and eaters of any age to the world of veggie cakes, cookies and desserts.

Feel free to play around with other winter squash varieties, from the gorgeous density of flesh found in kabocha squash to the playful strings of spaghetti squash. And then, there are courgettes or zucchini. They're not sweet, but that's also their strength – absorbent and bland, the inner white flesh of a courgette is the perfect vehicle for another flavour. Whether steamed, puréed or spiralised, they're simple to sweeten up, and very versatile for their decorative possibilities too. If you can find ones with yellow or pale green skins, they're best, as their flavour is milder and sweeter, and visually more in keeping with our ideas of dessert. The same goes for marrows, which are simply big courgettes.

Cucumbers are perhaps a different story, with their high water content. I'd suggest treating them instead as a source of liquid by first pulverising them in a blender to make 'sludge', and then using this as a humectant in recipes. In this way, cucumbers make a fantastic base for chia pudding or as the liquid component for raw yacon flour-based custard.

CELERY-LIKE VEGGIES
This is complicated, as I've delegated some members of the celery family to other categories, for example, carrots and celeriac roots are discussed in the Roots and Tubers section. Celeriac is simply the enlarged root of a variety of celery that's been bred for its bulbous root more than its upper parts. Celery has the same flavour profile, with a strange stringy stem that's juicy and more herby. De-string it and blend with coconut cream and chia seeds for an easy raw pudding; if this is steeped for a few hours it becomes custardy.

Fennel is in the same family – a triple vegetable, the base bulb has the lightest flavour, and softens with steaming. The stalks are the least accessible for desserts, due to their strong flavour and robust texture (though you could purée them and use as a paste for cookies or cakes), but don't let that deter you from using the leaves in a sweet vegetable dessert. The leaves have a distinctive fresh aniseed flavour, a welcome addition in many recipes.

PEAS AND BEANS
Peas are every child's favourite vegetable, because they're sweet! Smaller ones are sweeter, and frozen varieties are the sweetest by far, Chopped into rounds, green beans also add nubs of texture to cookies and cakes, not unlike dried fruit but less squishy. These aren't sweet, of course, but some other peas and beans are – mangetout, snow peas, and sugar snap peas, which are so-called because... they're sweet! Broad (fava) beans are less easy in terms of their sweetness, but they have a wonderful texture when cooked that can be flavoured and sweetened to create a dessert base. Likewise, edamame are simply immature soy beans, so it's possible to do fun dessert things with them. However, they're most versatile as fully matured soy beans, from which they can be used in flour form or as tofu.

ALLIUMS
Vidalia onions are a naturally sweet variety, but many onions can become perfectly sweet enough for a cake if they're caramelised to perfection, and glazed with honey. Hide them inside a cake batter. Shallots are also delicate and delicious, as are Walla Walla, Bermuda, and Maui onions. I draw the line at garlic, but maybe I will find a space even for garlic in the future; one of my favourite fruits is durian which has a complex array of natural compounds, including the main chemicals that make garlic taste like garlic. Durian is a tropical fruit popular throughout south-east Asia, and it's a member of the jackfruit family. It's very sweet and fatty, and let's just say it's an acquired taste that's like garlic custard. (I'll let you know when I find the garlic sweet spot – I'm confident that it exists.)

MUSHROOMS AND TRUFFLES
Umami is the essence of the savoury flavour experience, and mushrooms are full of umami, so they aren't an obvious friend of desserts. However, there's something special about savoury notes combining with sweetness. When you're cooking something savoury, a touch of maple syrup can bring out the flavours; likewise, if you're making dessert, adding a little portion of umami can show your tastebuds the way into the sweetness. Mushrooms do that. And they're also tender, delicately textured little sponges that are more than happy to soak up any flavours you care to marinate them in, and they come in such incredible shapes. Wood ear, enoki and maitake are naturally beautiful, and even white button mushrooms have a pretty profile when sliced. For this reason, mushrooms are as much about decoration as about taste. And don't forget truffles, they're a world of umami in themselves and a drizzle of truffle oil makes magic happen.

Opposite: Freshly shelled peas have natural sweetness, as do the members of the tasty squash family, from large pumpkins to small nutty-flavoured kuri squashes. Leafy greens like lettuces, mizuna, spinach and chard are definitely more usually associated with salads, but all have sweet potential.

LEAVES

Lettuces are generally sweeter than kale, and they're invariably more tender too. For this reason, I recommend trying out various lettuce varieties in dessert before you consider doing sweet things with kale. Butter lettuce is an obvious choice, being so tender, but also mizuna is fun, with its mustardy bite providing a note of spiciness that works well as a way to kick back from a sweet ingredient. I'm going to put rocket (arugula) into this category, as it works the same way, although in botanical terms, it's not a lettuce, but a member of the brassica family. It's confusing, but sometimes the culinary attributes of a vegetable don't align with its horticultural designation.

Spinach has some of this category-melding issue too, as it's technically related to buckwheat, as anyone can tell you who has grown it from seed. The seeds look identical to buckwheat, and the flowers it sprouts when it bolts yield pretty fronds of seeds at the end of summer that complete the cycle and look like a buckwheat crop. But spinach can be sweet! And tender. That's why people love it in savoury vegetable dishes, and will be open to sweet recipes with spinach too. Another deep leafy green that's great in sweet recipes is Swiss chard: this has a semi-soft texture and a mild flavour that's a little more challenging compared to bell peppers or parsnips, but which can be softened with cream and caramel. And chard comes in a rainbow of hues that are attractive both inside a tart or as a decorative topping.

Then, there are wild greens, like nettles. These are a traditional wild-crafted green vegetable that's under-used in any context, whether savoury or sweet. And finally, I wanted to mention the chicory and endive family, and say these slightly fuzzy leaves can add bitter notes that aren't obvious but perhaps still have a place, in the same way that gin is frequently embraced within a sweet cocktail.

FLOWERS

Flowers aren't vegetables, but then again, many vegetables do come from flowers that are edible, including peas and beans – artichokes are of course themselves giant flower buds, as are cauliflowers, broccoli and others of the cabbage family. Squash blossoms are a vegetable flower that's a culinary classic in some Mediterranean countries. Add to these other edible flowers, like rose petals and jasmine, and the palate can be extended elegantly. I like to include ingredients

Left: flowers aren't vegetables of course, but are considered acceptable as a cake ingredient, even though they are even less sweet – let's welcome both in our baking.

like fennel pollen in this grouping, as pollen is also from flowers. And while we're here, of course, the actual flowers of fennel are also wonderful, as are many of the other herbal flowers, from basil to thyme. They're often more pungent than leaves from the same plant, so a little goes a long way.

ASPARAGUS

This ancient vegetable has a classification all on its own. Luckily, there are numerous varieties to keep the group varied. Sweet, tender tips of asparagus are a natural friend to dessert recipes. Their pretty aesthetic and clean taste render them easy to use, and their versatile range of textures lends a special place to them. Steam for softness, grill for charred flavours, or simply chop and use raw for their pleasing crispness. Enjoy the wide spectrum of shades, from white to purple, and use them as much for decoration as for flavour and texture.

A side note about asparagus – some suggest that it isn't advisable in large quantities for those with or at risk of breast cancer; my personal view, as a survivor, is that it is a wonderful and healthy vegetable in moderation.

AVOCADOS

The star of the early 21st century, the avocado is an imposter, as it's technically a berry, each containing a single seed. However, as we're so used to serving it in a savoury context, it's included as a 'vegetable' in this cookbook, ready to wow you with simple creaminess in sweet recipes. Avocados are high in luscious fats (the good ones), and are my go-to first choice for anything creamy. Why only blend them with spices and salt when their flesh is an equally great vehicle for sweetness? Mash in anything at all, from cinnamon to chocolate. I've listed avocados as their own category, as the only other related edible ingredient are bay leaves. There are many different varieties that all have different textures, from the bumpy-skinned and ubiquitous Haas to the smooth, oily Bacon.

SPROUTED SEEDS AND BEANS

You can sprout pretty much any seed, bean or pulse. Lentils, broad beans, chickpeas, mung, oat groats, sunflower seeds. Anything that still has its shell intact can be gently coaxed into sprouting. Some tiny seed sprouts offer pretty tangles, like alfalfa or broccoli. Classic mung beansprouts crunch in your mouth like nothing else. They don't have a lot of flavour; with these it's all about the crispy bite and the shape. I recommend celebrating their juiciness by throwing them into your raw desserts.

Left: fiddlehead ferns are mystical vegetables from the forest. Only found in the wild, in regions that have cold winters, they are considered harbingers of spring.

SWEET CORN

This is obvious. It's called sweetcorn in the UK, because, it's sweet! Strange varieties have been developed to create strains for manufacturing high-fructose corn syrup, a basic building block of the evil empire, in my opinion. But, old-fashioned sweet corn is simply sweet, and it's a high-quality vegetable that's totally good to eat. Actually, to be entirely accurate, it's an oversized grain – a variety of maize. I've met lots of people who avoid sweet corn because they're scared of the genetically modified variety. However, GM corn is never sold as a vegetable – it's only ever sold after it's been processed into syrup, and is usually hidden in processed foods rather than being sold in any form as a stand-alone ingredient. So if you see sweet corn on the cob, or in cans or frozen, it's not been genetically modified, and it's perfect for adding to healthy vegetable cakes. Even better if it's also organic!

Adding some fresh crunchy kernels of sweet corn to a regular fruit salad is a fantastic way to introduce people to the idea of vegetables as a dessert ingredient. Explore the many heirloom varieties that Mexican, Peruvian and Bolivian farmers in particular have developed over the centuries. Some of the more beautiful varieties include the red, purple and speckled corns as well as the black, bronze, and multi-coloured Glass Gem Corn, which has a gem-like quality with translucent pink, purple, blue and orange kernels. Indescribably otherworldly, and worth growing from seed if you have the space, for their decorative possibilities as well as to be used in recipes.

AND FINALLY... FIDDLEHEAD FERNS

The signifier of spring in the places they grow, fiddlehead ferns have a brief annual window of seasonal availability, as they're never cultivated – they are only foraged naturally from the wild. They are NEVER eaten raw, as they contain a lot of tannins. Instead, simply boil some water and immerse the fiddlehead ferns for 3–5 minutes, depending on their size. Drain the water, or remove them with a slotted spoon, and immediately plunge them into very cold water to stop the cooking. They're ready to be used now, either directly eaten, or by frying or baking or any other method of preparation. They taste like asparagus mixed with hazelnuts and grass... and their gentle, very spring-like flavour is lovely in desserts. Their curling wonderousness is explored in the special galette-style tart on page 114.

DIETARY SYMBOLS
These abbreviations give at-a-glance guidance to what's in (or rather not in) the recipes.

NF nut-free

DF dairy-free

VG vegan

RW raw

SF refined sugar-free

GF gluten-free

PL paleo

Coconut Cream, Creamed Coconut, and Other Creamy Coconutty Things...

Coconuts aren't vegetables, of course, but I'm including this page about coconut cream as I use it frequently to make wonderful dairy-free cheesecakes, creamy toppings, and as an ingredient for baking. Commercial coconut creams vary, so I wanted to give some guidelines for choosing and using them. To start, there are two very different products available with confusingly similar names: coconut cream, and creamed coconut. (There's also a third product called 'cream of coconut', that's something else again.)

Coconut cream is a liquid sold in a can or a carton, and it has a similar consistency to double (heavy) cream, or whipping cream. It's made by cooking coconut meat with either water or coconut juice, and then straining it. You can buy it as full-fat or light, but I always recommend using the full-fat version for cakes, to ensure it will whip to the desired consistency.

Most brands of coconut cream also contain guar gum, which is a high-fibre natural additive made by milling guar beans. It promotes healthy internal flora, as you'd expect from a bean product, so it has a side-benefit of being good for you, as well as improving the consistency of the coconut cream. Guar gum has a stabilising effect on liquids, which means that it stops water and fats from separating, and it's also a thickener. I strongly recommend only using coconut cream that contains guar gum for this reason; creams that are simply coconut and water easily separate, and have a less appetising flavour and appearance. Guar gum is a permitted additive as it's simply made of milled beans, so it's possible to find organic coconut cream that contains guar gum. My favourite brands are Waitrose own-label organic in the UK, and Trader Joe's own label in the USA, but there are others you can try. Just choose a brand that contains guar gum.

With the exception of the Trader Joe brand (which I particularly love for its creaminess and thick consistency), coconut cream usually separates in the can. For this reason, I recommend storing the unopened can in the refrigerator beforehand,

then pouring off the separated liquid when it's opened. The harder cream can then be thinned to the desired thickness with the liquid to suit your recipe.

To make a simple frosting, pour off the liquid from a can of coconut cream and then whip the remaining solids with an electric hand mixer, thinning it with some of the reserved liquid until it resembles thick cream.

Coconut cream is typically sold in small 160ml/5½fl oz cans, or in standard 400ml/14fl oz cans. The measurements in this book refer to the whole of the canned cream, including liquid, unless otherwise stated. Another note on measurements: most cans are sold by liquid rather than weight, but in practice if a recipe asks for 175ml/6fl oz, then 175g/6oz is the same thing.

Creamed coconut is a totally different ingredient. Sold as a hard 200g/7oz block that looks rather like a bar of soap, this is the dehydrated meat of a fresh coconut, without any added liquid. A staple ingredient in Indian, West Indian, and South-East Asian cuisines, it is often grated into curries. It's 100% natural, and never contains any additional ingredients – it's pure coconut. When opened you will see a dense layer of dehydrated coconut meat, and a translucent layer of solid coconut oil. It's best to grate the entire block so these two elements are combined.

Creamed coconut works very differently to coconut cream, so they cannot be used interchangeably. That said, creamed coconut can also be used to make a delicious frosting for cakes, and a thinner icing to use as a glaze or drizzle. Simply grate a solid creamed coconut block using a box grater, and blend in a bowl with 2 tbsp boiling hot water, 1 tbsp maple syrup, and 50ml/2fl oz/¼ cup non-dairy milk. The consistency will be similar to cream cheese frosting, but vegan, refined sugar-free and paleo.

Cream of Coconut, by the way, is a completely different thing again. It's rare to find outside of the alcoholic mixer section, and is roughly half coconut milk and half sweetener, so not something to use if you're sensitive to refined sugar. Best kept for pina colada.

Cakes

There's nothing like a cake to announce a special occasion. Whether for a birthday party, the end of a beautiful dinner party, or a fancy afternoon tea, a cake shouts out "Let's Celebrate!" So what happens when your cake contains copious amounts of vegetables? What does it say if you present a sweet culinary creation that's full of carrots, radishes, cauliflower or kale? It says "Be creative, be daring and – eat this without guilt, it's healthy!" It lets your guests know you're inventive and open to new ideas, and shows them that you want to look after them enough to make a unique, never-had-that-before kind of a cake. Not just any old cake – a totally out-of-this-world cake. Enjoy your journey into a less-explored part of the culinary garden with these gloriously different and delectable vegetable treats.

Kale and Coconut Gâteau

A sweet gâteau, with dehydrated coconut and crisped kale topping a rich frosted layer cake, and a filling of deliciously moist massaged kale and coconut inside.

Kale is undeniably everywhere at the moment, but often it's not tenderised before it's served, so the texture isn't great. It's simple to fix this by massaging the kale before use, whether that's for a salad or for a cake like this one. It's a spectacular layered gâteau, flavoured with a gorgeous combination of coconut and crispy kale, and with macerated fronds of kale nestled into rich coconut-frosted goodness – plenty of naughty while still delivering on the nice. A true showstopper that tastes as good as it looks, and combining two fashionably favourite ingredients.

MAKES ONE 20CM/8IN CAKE, SERVES 8–10

15ml/1 tbsp coconut oil, warmed, plus extra for greasing

100g/3¾oz/1 cup coconut flour, plus extra for dusting

30g/1oz/2 cups shredded kale

125g/4½oz/generous 1 cup gluten-free plain (all-purpose) flour mix

7.5ml/1½ tsp baking powder

2.5ml/½ tsp guar gum

2.5ml/½ tsp pink or sea salt

225g/8oz/1 cup/2 sticks unsalted butter, at room temperature

300g/10oz/1¾ cups coconut sugar

5 eggs, at room temperature

250ml/8fl oz/1 cup coconut milk

7.5ml/1½ tsp organic coconut extract

For the filling and topping

400ml/14fl oz can of coconut cream, chilled

30ml/2 tbsp raw agave syrup

30g/1oz/½ cup desiccated raw (dry unsweetened macaroon-cut shredded) coconut

1 Preheat the oven to 170°C/325°F/Gas 3. Grease two 20cm/8in round cake tins (pans) with coconut oil, and dust them with the extra coconut flour.

2 Put the shredded kale into a small bowl, then coat your hands with the warmed coconut oil. Using strong pressure, squish the kale so that the juices come out of the leaves and they become naturally macerated. Keep doing this for about 3–4 minutes, until the kale has reduced to about half its volume. Set aside about a quarter to use as the decorative topping, and keep the rest to hand.

3 Sift the flours and baking powder into a large bowl with the guar gum and salt. In a separate bowl, cream the butter with the coconut sugar with an electric mixer on medium speed. Add the eggs one at a time, each with roughly a tablespoon of flour mixture.

4 When all of the eggs have been combined, add the coconut milk and 5ml/1 tsp of the extract, and keep whisking until smooth. Add the remaining flour mixture and whisk until it is all incorporated.

5 Gently fold in the kale using a wooden spoon or a spatula. Divide the cake batter equally between the two tins (pans), and bake for about an hour, until golden brown and a skewer inserted comes out clean. Allow to cool in the tins for 10 minutes before turning out on to a wire rack.

6 Next make the filling and topping. Open the chilled can of coconut cream and drain away any excess liquid, leaving the semi-solid white coconut cream. Using an electric hand whisk, whip this with 2.5 ml/½ tsp coconut extract and the agave until light and fluffy.

7 Place one cake on a platter, then spread half of the coconut cream filling over evenly. Sandwich the second cake on top, and spread with the rest of the cream.

8 Spread the remaining kale in a roasting pan and bake for a few minutes at 170°C/325°F/Gas 3 till just crisp. Cool for 5 minutes then sprinkle the roasted kale and shredded coconut over the cake and serve immediately.

Radish Pavlova

Aquafaba meringue topped with mandolin-slices of radish. For a lovely subtle floral flourish, you can decorate with rose petals and even radish 'roses' soaked in rose water.

There's a new magic ingredient, and it's beyond surprising. In fact, we've always known about it but never realised its potential. Once discarded as a waste product, the cooking liquid from a can of chickpeas has now found recognition as a wonder ingredient dubbed 'aquafaba' (or 'bean water') by the French chef Joel Roessel, and a food blogger by the name of Goose Wohlt. The liquid is the gloopy, creamy fibres of the beans, and acts similarly to egg whites. It's the ultimate vegan no-waste foodstuff. Now I often find myself buying cans of chickpeas and white beans purely for the aquafaba, and then making hummus so I don't waste the 'by-product' of the beans themselves! Simply strain the liquid from the can and whisk, to create a fabulous foam that forms the basis of an egg-free meringue.

1 Set the oven to 100°C/200°F/Gas ¼. Line a large baking sheet with baking parchment or use a silicone mat.

2 Using an electric whisk on high setting, beat the aquafaba until whipped to stiff glossy peaks, about 8 minutes. Whisk in the cream of tartar, guar gum and Versawhip (if using), and vanilla extract.

3 Sift the cornflour into a small bowl, and mix together with the sugar. Slowly add this mixture, one tablespoon at a time, to the aquafaba foam, still beating on high with the electric whisk. After about 2–3 minutes the ingredients will be combined, and the foam still firm.

4 Spread the foam onto the baking sheet, heaping it in the middle as it will spread out slightly. You could pipe the foam if you prefer a more formal look.

5 Bake for 2 hours, then turn the oven off and leave the meringue in the oven for another 5 hours.

(continued overleaf)

(NF) (DF) (VG) (GF)

MAKES ONE 20CM/8IN PAVLOVA, SERVES 6-8

- 175ml/6fl oz/²⁄₃ cup aquafaba i.e. the liquid from a no-salt can of chickpeas
- 1.5ml/¼ tsp cream of tartar (optional)
- 1.5ml/¼ tsp guar gum (optional)
- 1.5ml/¼ tsp Versawhip (optional)
- 2.5ml/½ tsp vanilla extract
- 50g/2oz/½ cup cornflour (cornstarch)
- 150g/5oz/¾ cup caster (superfine) sugar
- A bunch of fresh radishes, topped and tailed
- 30ml/2 tbsp raw agave syrup
- 5ml/1 tsp rose water (optional)
- 400ml/14fl oz can of coconut cream, chilled
- Mint sprigs and rose petals, to decorate

6 While the meringue is in the cooling oven, slice the radishes as thinly as possible using a mandolin. Soak the slices in a bowl with the agave and rose water, if using.

7 When you're nearly ready to serve the pavlova, open the chilled can of coconut cream and drain away the liquid (retaining it in a bowl as you will want to use some of it), leaving the thick semi-solid cream. Using an electric whisk, whip the cream, adding some of the reserved liquid little by little until the desired consistency is reached. It needs to be thick so it will stay on top of the pavlova.

8 Remove the meringue from the oven, spread with the whipped coconut cream and top with the macerated radishes. Decorate with mint sprigs and rose petals. As the meringue will start to moisten, serve immediately.

DECORATION IDEA
To decorate with radish 'roses', trim radishes and make vertical cuts three-quarters of the way through in a rose pattern, using a sharp knife. Put into a bowl of cold water infused with a little rose water, and soak in the refrigerator overnight. Drain well before using.

OPTIONAL INGREDIENTS
The cream of tartar, guar gum, and Versawhip are all optional ingredients. I've found that they add stability to the uncooked foam, and structure to the finished baked meringue, but they aren't necessary. Many people prefer their pavlova to have more crevices and cracks. Also, I usually recommend avoiding refined sugar but don't attempt to substitute it in this meringue – the chemistry won't work! This meringue is lovely with almond instead of vanilla extract, if you like, though it won't then be nut-free.

Cauliflower, Chocolate and Coconut Cake

Cauliflower is 'riced' and transformed into a super-moist cake with the fabulous flavour combination of coconut and chocolate. A maple coconut cream makes it even more special.

This delectable vegetable cake has an incredibly moist and fudgy texture, with a classic cake-like crumb and a topping of whipped coconut cream. It is a perfect entry-level recipe to introduce vegetable cakes to your family and friends, and to serve for a celebration. To 'rice' the cauliflower, I use a box grater, or pulse it in a food processor to make little rice-sized pieces. You can buy packs of pre-riced cauliflower but it's more nutritious to do yourself.

(NF) (DF) (VG) (SF) (GF) (PL)

MAKES ONE 20CM/8IN CAKE, SERVES 8

- 100ml/3½fl oz/scant ½ cup coconut oil
- 100ml/3½fl oz/scant ½ cup maple syrup
- 50g/2oz/¼ cup coconut sugar
- 150g/5¾oz chocolate, 100% cocoa solids (or 70% if you aren't strictly paleo)
- 2.5ml/½ tsp pink or sea salt
- 175ml/6fl oz/⅔ cup aquafaba i.e. the liquid from a can of chickpeas
- 150g/5oz/1½ cups coconut flour
- 4.5ml/¾ tsp bicarbonate of soda (baking soda)
- 400g/14oz/4 cups grated cauliflower (about 1 large head, cored), plus florets for decoration

For the frosting
- 400g/14oz/2 blocks solid creamed coconut
- 60ml/4 tbsp boiling water
- 45ml/3 tbsp maple syrup
- 120ml/4fl oz/½ cup coconut or non-dairy milk
- 1 carrot, for decoration

1 Preheat the oven to 190°C/370°F/Gas 5. Line the bottoms of two 20cm/8in round loose-based cake tins (pans) with baking parchment. The batter is quite oily so there's no need to grease non-stick tins (pans).

2 In a saucepan, heat the coconut oil until liquid and then mix in the maple syrup and coconut sugar. Heat for 2 minutes until bubbling and combined. Break in the chocolate, take the pan off the heat, and stir so it combines. Add the salt, and set aside.

3 In a bowl, whisk the aquafaba for 4 minutes with an electric hand mixer on the highest setting until it forms soft, white peaks. Fold in the chocolate mixture and then the flours, bicarbonate of soda and grated cauliflower.

4 Transfer the batter equally into the prepared cake tins and bake for 40 minutes until still moist but fairly firm in the centres. Allow to cool in the tins, then transfer to wire racks to cool completely, being careful as they are so squishy. Leave in the fridge overnight – this does improve the consistency and makes the cakes fudgy and cohesive.

5 The next day, grate the creamed coconut into a bowl, and, using a metal spoon, blend with 4 tbsp boiling water, the 3 tbsp maple syrup and the coconut milk to make a creamy frosting. Stand for 10 minutes to warm and combine, then blend again. (If you prefer, you can simply use canned coconut cream instead of the block and coconut milk, see page 21 for details.)

6 Removing the paper, set the first cake on a plate. Spread with coconut frosting then peel the paper from the second cake and place it on top. Cover with the rest of the frosting. Decorate with carrot ribbons (I use a vegetable peeler) and tiny cauliflower slices. This cake keeps for 4 days in an airtight container, and improves every day.

DECORATION IDEA
Top the cake with sweet, crisped cauliflower florets if you like. Place small slices on a baking sheet and drizzle with 15ml/1 tbsp of maple syrup. Bake in a 210°C/425°F/Gas 7 oven for 10 minutes then allow to cool before using.

Red Radicchio Cake

Purple leaves are baked in a gluten-free polenta sponge. With ingredients inspired by a classic salad, this is an adventurous cake, but one that will win you over with its ruby hues.

Lettuce, lemon and olive oil with yogurt; tarragon and black pepper to provide yet more salady nuance... reading through this recipe it does sound more unusual than it tastes! The warmth of cinnamon ties everything together to create a deliciously sweet cake with a subtle Greek flavour. It is a versatile and enjoyable creation that's perfect any time of day. Serve it with mint tea or Greek-style coffee for total Mediterranean immersion.

(NF) (DF) (SF) (GF)

MAKES ONE 20CM/8IN CAKE, SERVES 8

- 250ml/8fl oz/1 cup coconut yogurt, drained
- Zest and juice of ½ lemon
- 120ml/4fl oz/½ cup olive oil, plus extra to grease and drizzle
- 200g/8 oz radicchio leaves
- 3 eggs, beaten
- 150g/5oz/¾ cup coconut sugar
- 90g/3½oz/¾ cup gluten-free plain (all-purpose) flour mix
- 150g/5oz/1¼ cups polenta
- 45ml/3 tbsp dried tarragon
- 5ml/1 tsp ground cinnamon
- 1.5ml/¼ tsp ground black pepper
- 1.5ml/¼ tsp pink or sea salt
- 10ml/2 tsp baking powder
- Fresh tarragon sprigs, to decorate

1 If the coconut yogurt you're using isn't strained, measure it into a small bowl, and leave to stand for 10 minutes to allow the excess fluid to separate. Preheat the oven to 180°C/350°F/Gas 4. Grease a 20cm/8in round spring-form cake tin (pan) with olive oil.

2 Mix the lemon zest and juice with the olive oil in a non-metallic mixing bowl to make a dressing.

3 Keeping the prettier small leaves for the topping, very finely chop about half the radicchio leaves with a sharp knife, until the pieces are small but still definable in order to add the texture when baked – about roughly the size of sunflower seeds. Alternatively, use a food processor to do this. Add the chopped radicchio to the dressing.

4 Discard any excess whey from the yogurt, and then add the yogurt to the radicchio mixture and stir together with a spatula. Add the beaten eggs, and combine again. Finally, add all the rest of the ingredients, and mix well using the spatula.

5 Transfer the mix into the tin, pushing some whole radicchio leaves into the mixture on top, and bake for about 35–40 minutes, until a skewer inserted into the cake comes out clean. The exact baking time will depend on the moisture from the radicchio and the yogurt.

6 Leave to cool in the tin before turning out by running a spatula around the edges of the tin and releasing the spring-form clasp.

7 Decorate with an extra drizzle of olive oil, radicchio leaves and a few sprigs of fresh tarragon.

COOK'S TIP

I love the taste of the little pieces of radicchio. Somehow, they remain crunchy after the cake is baked and add a surprisingly fun texture. This recipe works equally well with any type of lettuce, including baby greens. For maximum crunch, I recommend using Romaine lettuce, or iceberg provides a great texture, with a less 'green' flavour. This is a whimsical creation, serving up salad as a cake!

Asparagus Sesame Cake

Roasted spears of asparagus swim upstream through a Japanese-inspired sweet barley sponge infused with sesame, matcha, chilli flakes and shiso.

This cake has so many flavours to bump into, from the heat of the chilli to the fragrance of shiso. If you can't find shiso, a type of basil widely used in Japan, it's easily replaced with fresh Italian basil.

I've carefully considered the textural elements to this recipe, from the density and moisture of the crumb to the soft fibrous surprise of the asparagus spears that they hide. Of course, that's also what makes this a springtime cake, as it's always best to eat asparagus during its seasonal appearance. It's a cleansing vegetable, great for moving sluggish wintry feelings out of the body. Black sesame acts as a great blood tonic, and helps restore vitality. But these points are by the by; the main reason to invest a weekend-hour on this recipe is that it's a truly delicious loaf cake, and even better eaten with a cup of matcha tea.

SF

MAKES ONE 23CM/9IN LOAF CAKE, SERVES 8–10

- 8–10 thin spears of fresh asparagus
- 30ml/2 tbsp black sesame seeds
- 250ml/8fl oz/1 cup water
- 225g/8oz/1 cup/2 sticks butter, at room temperature, plus a little extra for greasing
- 200g/7oz/1 cup coconut sugar
- 3 eggs
- 125g/4½oz/generous 1 cup barley flour
- 125g/4½oz/generous 1 cup plain (all-purpose) flour
- 15ml/1 tbsp matcha powder
- 15ml/1 tbsp chilli flakes
- 10ml/2 tsp vanilla extract
- 5ml/1 tsp baking powder
- 2.5ml/½ tsp almond extract
- 1.5ml/¼ tsp pink or sea salt
- 6–8 fresh shiso leaves, centre spines removed and finely cut

1 Grease a 23 x 13cm/9 x 5in loaf tin (pan) with butter, and line with parchment paper. Cut the asparagus spears to size so they fit into the tin, discarding the base of the stems. Put the asparagus into a steam basket, and steam in a lidded pan of boiling water for 5 minutes, until tender.

2 Place the black sesame seeds and the measured water in a blender, and process on the highest setting for about 1 minute, until a smooth 'milk' has formed. Set aside.

3 Preheat the oven to 180°C/350°F/Gas 4. Using an electric whisk, cream together the butter and sugar, then add the eggs, one at a time, and mix to a batter. Add all the remaining ingredients except the shiso. Whisk in half of the sesame milk to combine, then add the rest and whisk again.

4 Place a few shiso leaves and asparagus pieces in the base of the tin. Cover with half the batter, then another layer of asparagus and shiso. Cover with the rest of the batter, smooth down, and top with 2 more shiso leaves and a final asparagus spear sliced in half.

5 Bake for 1 hour, until it's golden brown and a skewer inserted into the middle comes out clean. Leave to cool in the pan before turning out to serve.

Carrot and Coriander Cake

Carrot cake is everyone's favourite vegetable cake. The original California hippy classic, updated to make a simple, quick and very nice everyday bake – with a twist!

Despite having a reputation for being healthy, most carrot cake recipes are laden with sugar and low on carrots. This version bucks that trend, and also draws inspiration from another 1960s' classic – carrot and coriander soup. Carrots, coriander and fennel all share the same botanical family, which includes parsnips and dill. For this reason, feel free to switch out the carrots for parsnips, or the coriander for dill – or both! (And serve it with fennel tea, as the natural choice to bring out the coriander notes.) There's a reason I've suggested using both whole and ground coriander, as the little bursts of whole seeds intensify the taste.

DF SF GF PL

MAKES 6 LARGE OR 15 SMALL SQUARES

2 medium eating apples, such as Pink Lady

70g/2¾oz fresh coriander (cilantro) leaves

100ml/3½fl oz/scant ½ cup coconut oil, plus extra for greasing

120ml/4fl oz/½ cup raw agave syrup

2 eggs, separated

500g/1¼lb carrots, grated

5ml/1 tsp ground coriander

5ml/1 tsp whole coriander seeds

100g/3¾oz roughly ground walnuts, plus pieces for decoration

100g/3¾oz/1 cup cornflour (cornstarch)

200g/7oz/1 block solid creamed coconut , grated

50ml/2fl oz/¼ cup almond milk

15ml/1 tbsp maple syrup

1 Place the whole apples in a pan, cover with boiling water and simmer for 20 minutes. Drain and allow to cool slightly then core and blend in a food processor or blender with 50g/2oz of the fresh coriander until pulped. Or just mash with a fork, or push through a sieve.

2 Preheat the oven to 180°C/350°F/Gas 4. Grease and line a 20 x 25cm/8 x 10in baking tin (pan) with the extra oil.

3 Transfer the apple mixture to a bowl and mix in the coconut oil, agave syrup, and egg yolks. Whisk for 1 minute, then stir in the grated carrots and then the ground and whole coriander seeds.

4 In a separate bowl, whisk the egg whites for 3 minutes until peaks form. Fold into the carrot and apple mixture and add the ground walnuts. Fold the cornflour thoroughly into the mixture and then transfer to the prepared tin.

5 Bake for 1 hour and 25 minutes, until firm. Allow to cool completely in the tin before turning the cake out.

6 In a bowl, mix the grated coconut with 30ml/2 tbsp boiling water, the almond milk and maple syrup. Blend together with the back of a spoon until smooth. (If you prefer, you can use canned coconut cream instead of the block and almond milk and syrup, see page 21 for details.)

7 Spread the cake with the coconut frosting, then decorate with the remaining fresh coriander and walnut pieces. Cut into squares and serve.

Okra Cacao Bundt Cake

Okra can faze many, even as a side vegetable – let alone in a cake! Yet, this sweet bake might actually be the key to a wider acceptance of this unusual vegetable.

Okra is enjoyed in many cuisines, from the Louisiana bayou to Pondicherry. However, nobody traditionally eats it in cake, and that seems a missed opportunity, as it infuses cakes with the moisture we often crave. Especially in a dense bundt cake.

Freshly ground cardamom is always more fragrant if you have the time. Simply squeeze the whole pods to release the seeds, and discard the outer wrapping. Grind the spice using a pestle and mortar, or an electric spice grinder. The pods each contain around a dozen seeds, and it takes about 60 seeds to make a teaspoon of powder, so that's roughly 5 pods per teaspoon. Likewise, if you'd like more emphasis on the chocolate notes, feel free to be heavy-handed on the cacao. The given amount is great for a subtle background flavour and a rich colour, but if you like a particularly gooey, chocolatey cake, why not fold some broken chocolate into the mix with the aquafaba. Either way, the okra will sing the starring aria in this epically operatic cake. Serve warm or cool.

MAKES ONE CAKE, SERVES 8–10

200ml/7fl oz/1 cup coconut oil, plus extra for greasing

100ml/3½fl oz/scant ½ cup raw agave syrup

100g/3¾oz/½ cup coconut sugar

Zest and juice of ½ lemon

500ml/17fl oz/generous 2 cups coconut milk

250g/9oz/2 cups coconut flour

5ml/1 tsp bicarbonate of soda (baking soda)

30ml/2 tbsp unsweetened cacao powder

Pinch of pink or sea salt and ground black pepper

Seeds of 5 cardamom pods, ground

175ml/6fl oz/⅔ cup aquafaba ie the liquid from a can of chickpeas

400g/14oz okra

Desiccated raw (dry unsweetened macaroon-cut shredded) coconut, to decorate

1 Preheat the oven to 190°C/370°F/Gas 5 and grease a 2.4-ltr/4.2-pint/10-cup bundt tin (pan) or silicone mould,

2 Melt the coconut oil in a large pan, then mix in the agave syrup and coconut sugar and bubble up over a medium heat until combined. Stir in the lemon juice and milk. Bring to the boil, then mix in the coconut flour, bicarbonate of soda and cacao powder. Season with salt, black pepper and ground cardamom. Remove from the heat and allow to cool.

3 Whip the aquafaba for 6–7 minutes using an electric whisk, until white and in soft peaks. Fold the aquafaba into the rest of the ingredients in the pan.

4 Trim the okra, and then slice a third of them lengthways. Fill the bottom of the bundt tin with the sliced okra, skin-side down, then transfer half of the cake batter into the tin, covering the bottom and sides in a layer. Fill the bundt tin with the remaining whole okra and follow with a layer of the remaining cake mixture, smoothing the top with the back of a spoon.

5 Bake for 45 minutes until firm to touch. Allow to cool slightly, then turn out on to a plate. Serve topped with lemon zest and coconut (and dill fronds, if you like).

Godzilla Cake

A round coconut cake with a whole Romanesco baked inside, so that the top of it emerges like a creature from a prehistoric lagoon. The slices are wonderfully graphic and striking!

Is this a cake, or a sculpture? Is it a dessert, or a B-movie? When it comes to looks, no vegetable beats Romanesco. This Italian staple is an heirloom variety of brassica that tastes pretty much the same as a cauliflower, but has the great visual attribute of Fibonacci spirals. Rising out of this flourless coconut cake, the vegetable is like a magnificent monster – hence the name. Beautiful, alien, and utterly comic-book, this sweet creation is a winner for anybody who enjoys sci-fi movies, graphic novels, or mathematics. I have never met anyone who didn't gasp in wonder.

MAKES ONE 20CM/8IN CAKE, SERVES 6–8

- 100g/3¾oz/½ cup/1 stick butter, at room temperature, plus extra for greasing
- 50ml/2fl oz/¼ cup coconut oil, for greasing
- 1 Romanesco cauliflower
- 120g/4¼oz/2¼ cups desiccated raw (dry unsweetened macaroon-cut shredded) coconut
- 120g/4¼oz/⅔ cup coconut sugar
- 3 eggs
- 2.5ml/½ tsp ground cinnamon
- 2.5ml/½ tsp ground cardamom
- 5ml/1 tsp baking powder
- 1.5ml/¼ tsp pink or sea salt
- Zest of 1 lemon
- 50g/2oz/½ cup cornflour (cornstarch)
- 50ml/2fl oz/¼ cup maple syrup

1 Preheat the oven to 180°C/350°F/Gas 4. Grease a 20cm/8in springform round baking tin (pan) with the extra butter, and set aside.

2 Remove the leaves from the Romanesco. With coconut oil, grease the bottom of another baking tin that's big enough for the Romanesco to stand in, and place it in, on its flat base. Oil the Romanesco liberally, rubbing into the crevices, and put into the hot oven to bake for 25–30 minutes.

3 Meanwhile, make the cake batter by adding the desiccated coconut, coconut sugar, eggs, spices, baking powder, salt and lemon zest to the butter in a food processor. Process the ingredients, starting on the lowest speed and slowly raising the speed as high as the batter will allow, scraping down the sides of the bowl with a spatula. After a few minutes, when everything is smooth, add the cornflour and process again to combine.

4 Remove the Romanesco from the oven, and transfer it to the centre of the springform cake tin. Pour over the oil that's left in the bottom of the tin it's been cooking in, so the Romanesco is basted.

5 Transfer the batter from the food processor to the cake tin, pouring it around the Romanesco to carefully avoid getting any batter on the vegetable top, but to cover the base of the tin. The Romanesco will rise out like Godzilla.

6 Bake for 25–30 minutes, until golden brown and the edges are starting to brown.

7 Remove from the oven and immediately pour the maple syrup over the Romanesco top that's still revealed in the centre of the cake.

8 Allow to cool completely before running a knife around the sides of the tin, and then removing the springform sides. Place on a platter or cake stand to serve it whole at the table, with a pitcher of pouring coconut cream alongside. The effect is most dramatic with a super-large Romanesco!

Tomato and Almond Cake

A flourless ring cake made with cherry tomatoes, ground almonds and spices. Moist and dense, it has a sweet, distinctive and almost persimmon-like flavour.

This has a similar pleasurable roasted note to a persimmon dessert, but with more acidity, and depending on the variety of tomato, it also has more sweetness. Choose true cherry tomatoes if you can find them, rather than the plum cherry tomatoes that are more often found in stores. The smaller and rounder cherry tomatoes are closer to the wild varieties, and they are sweeter, as well as containing more nutrients. If you're growing your own cherry tomatoes, I suggest trying chocolate cherries, as their dark brown colour doesn't give them any chocolate notes, but does produce a wonderfully complex and sweet tomato that's perfect for this cake, as well as being welcome in pretty much any other recipe.

If you like, serve the finished cake with an additional creamy maple-coconut glaze. And if you make this in a shaped bundt tin rather than a plain ring tin, the glaze will drip along the grooved lines, for a fantastic visual effect, This really is a lovely cake.

MAKES ONE 23CM/9IN CAKE, SERVES 8–10

30ml/2 tbsp coconut oil, for greasing

30ml/2 tbsp coconut flour, for dusting

600g/1lb 6oz/2 US pints cherry tomatoes

4 eggs

320g/11oz/2¼ cups coconut sugar

575g/1lb 4oz/5 cups ground almonds

10ml/2 tsp baking powder

12.5ml/2½ tsp ground cinnamon

7.5ml/1½ tsp ground cardamom

5ml/1 tsp ground nutmeg

5ml/1 tsp ground ginger

2.5ml/½ tsp pink or sea salt

For the glaze (optional)

200ml/7fl oz/scant 1 cup coconut milk

15ml/1 tbsp maple syrup

1.5ml/¼ tsp pink or sea salt

1 If you are making the glaze, prepare it ahead by mixing the coconut milk, maple syrup and salt in a pan. Turn the heat down to medium-low and cook uncovered for about 15 minutes, whisking regularly. Pour the condensed glaze into a bowl and leave to cool, then chill in the refrigerator for at least 2 hours, where it will thicken.

2 To make the cake, start by oiling a 20cm/8in ring or bundt tin (pan) or silicone mould, using melted coconut oil, making sure to oil well, and paying attention to the bottom of the tin in particular. Using a sieve or strainer, finely dust the inside of the tin with the coconut flour, keeping the coating as even as possible, and avoiding clumps. Invert the tin and tap to remove excess flour. Preheat the oven to 190°C/375°F/Gas 5.

3 I like to have the tomatoes congregate at the bottom (which will become the top!) but if you prefer you could have tomato integrated within the cake, in which case cut them into small chunks of around 1.5cm/¼in and mix them all into the batter at the end of step 4.

4 In a large mixing bowl, beat the eggs with the coconut sugar using a fork. Add the ground almonds, baking powder, and all of the spices and salt, and combine with a spatula, working quickly.

5 Line the tin with the tomatoes, then pour over the batter. Transfer to the oven and bake for 40 minutes, or until a skewer inserted into the middle comes out clean.

6 Fold a dish cloth in two and, placing it on the drainer, drench it in boiling water so that it is steaming. Invert the tin over the steaming dish cloth, and allow the cake to steam for about 10 minutes.

7 Carefully lift and tap the tin over a cooling rack to release the cake. Once the cake has cooled, transfer it to a serving platter.

8 If you are serving with cold coconut glaze, drizzle it over the cake or present it alongside for pouring.

Gidget's Gâteau

Fresh, raw tender salad in between layers of gluten-free and egg-free pancake. Frosted with sweet hummus, and creamy chocolate avocado...

Yes, you did just read that.

This is a vegan cake (please substitute the honey if you're not a honey-eater). It's made out of salad and chickpeas, with a touch of raw cacao. It's the healthiest cake anybody has ever eaten. I mean, it's made out of salad!

It is a visual 'wow!' dessert cake. It's named for my friend Gidget, who was fighting cancer when I started writing this book, and has the all-clear now. She ate a LOT of fresh greens and salad, as well as antioxidant-rich raw cacao and nutrient-dense avocados. Gidget deserves a cake to be named Gidget, and this is the one. She's an unconventional free spirit living in the mountains in California.

This recipe is absolutely the kind of activity to set aside a Sunday afternoon to do. It's fiddly, and it's silly, but you know what, it really does taste fantastic, and the crunch of the greens is a foil for the stickiness of the pancakes, and the creamy avocado layer.

This is the cake to serve to anyone who is careful about what they eat, or has allergies. It's not 100% raw because of the (egg-free, gluten-free) pancakes, but they're so fun, I'll bet everyone will want to try a piece.

DF VG SF GF

SERVES 6-8

For the sweet hummus layer

- 400ml/14fl oz can of no-salt organic chickpeas, with the liquid reserved for the pancakes
- ½ red (bell) pepper, deseeded and chopped
- 50g/2oz/¼ cup almond butter
- 50ml/2fl oz/¼ cup olive oil
- 2.5ml/½ tsp vanilla extract
- Zest and juice of ½ orange
- 50ml/2fl oz/¼ cup clear honey or maple syrup

For the chocolate avocado layer

- 1 ripe avocado
- 30ml/2 tbsp raw cacao powder
- 15ml/1 tbsp clear honey or maple syrup
- 2.5ml/½ tsp ground cinnamon
- 1.5ml/¼ tsp vanilla extract
- Zest and juice of ¼ orange

For the salad dressing

- 30ml/2 tbsp olive oil
- 30ml/2 tbsp clear honey or maple syrup
- Zest and juice of ¼ orange

For the salad filling

- 115g/4oz tender salad greens, such as butter lettuce, baby lettuces, baby spinach, mizuna and pea shoots
- 115g/4oz ripe baby plum or cherry tomatoes, halved
- 50g/2oz alfalfa sprouts
- 1 beefsteak tomato, sliced

For the pancakes

- 100g/3¾oz/1 cup chickpea flour
- 5ml/1 tsp ground cinnamon
- 2.5ml/½ tsp baking powder
- 175ml/6fl oz/⅔ cup aquafaba i.e. the liquid from the can of chickpeas used above
- 50ml/2fl oz/¼ cup olive oil, for frying

(continued overleaf)

1 To make the sweet hummus layer, open the can of chickpeas. Carefully drain the cooking liquid into a medium bowl and set aside.

2 Put the chickpeas into a blender along with the red pepper, almond butter, olive oil, vanilla and orange zest, and the honey or maple syrup. Blend on low.

3 Drizzle the orange juice in, little by little, until the desired consistency is reached. You probably won't need all of the juice. Scrape the sides of the blender using a spatula, and raise the speed to medium. When smooth, transfer the sweet hummus into a bowl and set aside.

4 To make the chocolate avocado layer, halve the avocado, and twist to remove the stone or pit. Scrape the flesh into a bowl. Add all of the other ingredients, and mash together with a fork, blending well. Cream together until there are no lumps visible, and it's a creamy consistency.

5 In a jug or cup, mix up the dressing ingredients. In a medium bowl, toss the mixed tender greens in the dressing to coat them well. Leave the tomatoes and alfalfa undressed, but in separate bowls ready to assemble.

6 To make the pancakes, sift the chickpea flour, cinnamon and baking powder together in a bowl and set aside.

7 Using an electric beater on medium, whisk a third of the aquafaba (the chickpea liquid that you set aside when you made the sweet hummus recipe). Beat the liquid for about 3 minutes, to soft peaks, not to super-stiff peaks. You want to see the ribbons from the whisks, and foam, but not enough foam to make meringues.

8 Using a spatula or a wooden spoon, fold the flour mixture into the whipped aquafaba liquid. Add the rest of the aquafaba a little at a time so that it combines to make a pancake batter. You probably won't need to add all of it to make a good pancake batter consistency.

9 Coat the bottom of a 25cm/10in frying pan with a tablespoon of olive oil. Fry the batter in four equal portions, flipping each pancake with the help of a fish slice or spatula. Cook each of the four pancakes on both sides until golden brown, then set aside on a rack to cool completely.

10 To assemble the cake, on a large platter (at least 30cm/12in), place one of the pancakes to form a base. Spread the pancake with some of the sweet hummus mixture, roughly 1cm/½in deep. Cover with the tender greens.

11 Top with pancake number two. Spread this pancake with some of the chocolate avocado mixture, roughly 1cm/½in deep. Cover with halved cherry tomatoes.

12 Spread the third pancake with the remaining sweet hummus mixture, roughly 1cm/½in deep, and place on top of the cherry tomatoes. Cover with the alfalfa sprouts.

13 Spread the rest of the chocolate avocado mixture on the fourth pancake. Carefully place on top of the cake. Decorate with extra sliced tomato and sprigs of peashoot or other salad greens. Serve immediately while it is fresh.

Cheesecakes

Cheesecakes have had a bit of a comeback in recent years, with new plant-based versions on the menu at raw restaurants, and the once-ubiquitous classic New York-style cheesecake being challenged by a line-up of new-fangled contenders that don't contain any cheese at all. Yes – this is a chapter full of cheesecakes that don't actually have any cheese in any of them.

Take the magnificent Beetroot Cheesecake, for example, made from beetroot and cashew nuts. While there's a little butter in the base, it's almost dairy-free. This is what many of us crave these days: something that's light on the dairy, and containing more fresh, healthy ingredients. This cheesecake is also gorgeous to behold, like a dessert lifted out of a fin-de-siècle painting.

The Fennel Pistachio Cheesecake is totally vegan, with a sophisticated absinthe and pollen note making it fit for a wedding. And then there's the Sunchoke Cheesecakes with Hazelnuts and Orange Zest, this time built with tofu and steamed sunchokes. And more liquor!

The Pumpkin Ginger Cheesecake is inspired by Japan, with pumpkin purée, coconut cream and silken tofu mingling with ginger and sunflower seeds. Or Cashew Rocket-Powered Cheesecake, sweetened with medjool dates and honey, and whipped up in no time at all. And finally, there's my recipe for a cheesecake made from purple cabbage, and named after Prince. Because someone had to do it, right?

Beetroot Cheesecake

Candied beetroots in a beetroot reduction on top of a creamy cashew mixture that contains – yes, more beetroots! This is an intensely coloured cheesecake.

The cookie crumb crust is made from scratch, and the cheesecake layer is based on cashews, so while this isn't a vegan cake, it's much lower on dairy than most cheesecakes.

Beyond that, there's nothing to say except that this celebration of the splendidly-hued beetroot is truly gorgeous to behold. Ruby. Garnet. Pure blood-red love on a cakestand.

MAKES ONE 23CM/9IN CHEESECAKE, SERVES 8–10

For the topping

250ml/8fl oz/1 cup beetroot juice

15ml/1 tbsp maple syrup

2.5ml/½ tsp vanilla extract

225g/8oz peeled and steamed beetroots (beets), halved but leaves intact

For the base

80g/3oz/⅓ cup/¾ stick cold butter, cut into pieces

100g/3¾oz/1 cup wholemeal (whole-wheat) flour

60g/2oz/⅔ cup rolled oats

30ml/2 tbsp coconut sugar

For the filling

450g/1lb peeled and steamed beetroots (beets)

225g/8oz/2 cups unroasted cashew nuts, soaked overnight

100ml/3½fl oz/scant ½ cup coconut oil, warmed, plus extra for greasing

Juice of 1 lemon

75ml/2½fl oz/⅓ cup maple syrup

1 First, make the topping. Boil the beetroot juice and maple syrup in a small uncovered pan for about 15 minutes until reduced to half of the original volume.

2 Add the vanilla, then pour the hot liquid over the halved beetroots in a shallow bowl. Set aside to marinate and cool to room temperature.

3 Preheat the oven to 180°C/350°F/Gas 4. Grease a 23cm/9in springform cake tin (pan) with a little coconut oil.

4 To make the base, in a large bowl, rub the butter into the flour, oats and coconut sugar to make big crumbs. Loosely press into the tin, and bake for 10 minutes, until lightly golden. Set the base aside to cool.

5 Meanwhile, little by little, blend all of the filling ingredients in a high-speed blender until creamy. This will be best achieved in a few batches, using a spatula to make sure everything is blended. Transfer the filling on to the crumb base and smooth with a spoon, then place in the freezer.

6 Take out of the freezer after about 20 minutes, and remove from the springform tin. Place on a serving platter.

7 Arrange the macerated beetroots decoratively on the cheesecake, pour over their syrup liquid, and serve at room temperature.

Fennel Pistachio Cheesecake

A luscious vegan cheesecake with delicate fennel and almond butter swirl, decorated with pale fennel fronds and pollen.

Perfect for a special occasion, the pistachio base and absinthe make this cheesecake luxurious enough to be placed on a pedestal as an artisanal wedding cake, served with absinthe or a glass of champagne. Fennel pollen, made from the dried heads of the flowers, is nicknamed the spice of angels.

There's not enough absinthe in this cake to do anything more than flavour it, so I don't think it's a problem for children to have a sliver at a wedding, for example. Vanilla extract probably has an equal amount of alcohol in it as this teaspoon of absinthe, but the flavour is special and unexpected, and lifts the fennel notes to a whole new level.

You can also make this cheesecake with peanut butter, and I also really like sunflower butter, with its lighter feel.

MAKES ONE 23CM/9IN CHEESECAKE, SERVES 8–10

For the base

- 115g/4oz/1 cup shelled unsalted pistachio nuts
- 1.5ml/¼ tsp pink or sea salt
- 200g/7oz/1 cup stoned (pitted) firm dried dates (not medjool)

For the filling

- 1 small fennel bulb, bottom only, chopped roughly
- 180g/6¼oz/1½ cups unroasted cashew nut pieces, soaked overnight in the refrigerator
- 80g/3¼oz/⅓ cup coconut oil, melted, plus extra for greasing
- 120ml/4fl oz/½ cup maple syrup
- Zest and juice of 1 lemon
- 400ml/14fl oz can of coconut cream, chilled (see step 4)

For the fennel swirl

- 30ml/2 tbsp almond butter, or other seed or nut butter
- 5ml/1 tsp absinthe, alternatively Pastis, Sambuca, or Ouzo would also work well
- Pinch of pink or sea salt
- Fennel fronds, roughly chopped
- 5ml/1 tsp olive oil
- 5ml/1 tsp fennel pollen

1 Grease a 23cm/9in springform cake tin (pan).

2 To make the base, process the pistachio nuts and salt together on low until ground into a flour. Next process the dates in a food processor on low until it forms a ball, but not a paste, with the little rice-sized pieces still visible.

3 In a bowl, combine the dates and pistachio mixtures together using your fingers to squish and form a dough. Press into the bottom of the springform tin, and put in the freezer while you prepare the filling.

4 Process the fennel bulb, drained cashew nuts, coconut oil, maple syrup, lemon juice and zest in a blender. Remove the can of coconut cream from the fridge and drain away the liquid (you can keep this in the fridge for another use), then measure out 160ml/5½fl oz/¾ cup of the solid cream – this will be most of the can. Add this to the blender, and blend again to combine all the filling ingredients. Transfer this mixture to the cake tin, and smooth over the base using a spatula.

5 Next, make the swirl dressing by combining the almond butter, absinthe and salt in a bowl or cup using the back of a fork. Add the chopped fennel fronds and olive oil, and combine with the fork to make a dressing. Pour the mixture over the centre of the cake, and swirl with the fork, making sure not to mix it in too much, but allowing it to look decoratively rough.

6 Cover the cheesecake with baking parchment, being careful to cover the whole cheesecake, but not so firmly that the filling is displaced.

7 Freeze for 4–6 hours, then remove the parchment, remove the springform tin, and set on a serving platter. Bring to room temperature before serving, which will take about an hour set on the counter.

8 Finish by sprinkling the pollen on top, concentrating it roughly on the centre, graduating out less and less towards the edges.

Sunchoke Vegan Cheesecake with Hazelnuts and Orange Zest

Another white cheesecake, this time containing sunchokes blended with tofu to make a purée, which is spread over a light hazelnut base infused with orange zest and sage.

Steamed sunchokes (otherwise known as Jerusalem artichokes) are hidden inside a creamy cheesecake layer. The sage and hazelnuts in the base pop against the orange notes, making this a lovely warm autumn dessert for the more curious people in your life. It's tinged with alcohol due to the orange liqueur in the filling, but just a teaspoonful. Individual cheesecakes are fun for a dinner party, or make one large cake for a more informal gathering.

MAKES 6–8 SMALL OR ONE LARGE CHEESECAKE

For the base

125g/4½ oz/generous 1 cup gluten-free plain (all-purpose) flour mix

50g/2oz/¼ cup/½ stick unsalted butter, plus extra for greasing

115g/4oz/1 cup ground hazelnuts

60ml/4 tbsp coconut sugar

Zest of ½ orange

7.5ml/1½ tsp dried ground sage

1.5ml/¼ tsp pink or sea salt

For the filling

5ml/1 tsp orange liqueur, such as Triple Sec, Curaçao, Grand Marnier or Cointreau

Juice of 1 orange

60ml/4 tbsp arrowroot

175g/6oz/1 cup sunchokes (Jerusalem artichokes), peeled and steamed

5cm/2in turmeric root, steamed

160ml/5½fl oz/generous ⅔ cup raw agave syrup

450g/1lb firm silken tofu (Japanese-style)

2.5ml/½ tsp pink or sea salt

For the coulis

400g/14oz/generous 2 cups sunchokes (Jerusalem artichokes), peeled and steamed

30ml/2 tbsp coconut sugar

7.5ml/1½ tsp dried ground sage

2.5ml/½ tsp orange liqueur, such as Triple Sec, Curaçao, Grand Marnier or Cointreau

Zest of ½ orange, plus strips for decorating

1 Grease individual moulds or a 23cm/9in springform cake tin (pan). To make the base, in a large bowl, rub the flour and butter together to form loose crumbs, then stir in the ground nuts and remaining ingredients, using your fingers to combine.

2 Press the mixture into the bottom of the moulds or tin and chill in the refrigerator for at least 20 minutes. Preheat the oven to 180°C/350°F/Gas 4.

3 Bake the base for 12–15 minutes, until it's cookie-like in colour and smells wonderful. Allow to cool while you make the filling. Reduce the oven to 150°C/300°F/Gas 2.

4 In a jug or cup, mix the orange liqueur, juice and arrowroot with a fork until combined. In a blender or food processor, blend the cooked sunchokes, turmeric root, agave syrup, tofu and salt. Transfer to a bowl and add the arrowroot mixture, and stir with a spatula to combine.

5 Wrap the outside of the moulds or springform tin tightly with heavy-duty foil so that the seams are all water-tight. Spoon the filling mixture into the moulds or tin. Set the moulds or tin inside a large roasting pan, and then pour in just-boiled water to come halfway up their sides.

6 Bake for 45 minutes until the centre of the cheesecakes are still not set but the sides are firm when the moulds are gently shaken. Allow to keep gently cooking in the oven for another 40 minutes. Remove from the oven and from the roasting pan and leave to cool before chilling in the refrigerator overnight.

7 To make the coulis, blend all of the ingredients together and strain through a sieve or strainer.

8 When ready to serve, bring the cheesecakes to room temperature, remove from the moulds or tin (pan) and decorate with strips of orange zest. Serve with the coulis spooned over or separately in a jug for guests to pour at the table.

Cashew Rocket-Powered Cheesecake

Fresh rocket – also called arugula – is blended with soaked cashew to make a vivid green filling, and also with medjool dates as a topping for this big, yet easy, showstopper.

This is an entry-level dessert to make, so it's a good choice to make with children, teenagers, or adults who don't have much experience in the kitchen. It contains a lot of nuts, so it's rich, and a little goes a long way. The colours are fun together, yet it's elegant enough to serve in any situation where there are people who are open to eating greens in their cheesecake.

The peppery bite of the rocket is totally softened by all of the sweetness surrounding it, and lends a lovely punctuation to the dates and honey.

(DF) (RW) (SF) (GF) (PL)

MAKES ONE 23CM/9IN CHEESECAKE, SERVES 8-10

For the base

75g/3oz/½ cup walnut pieces

75g/3oz/½ cup macadamia nuts

75g/3oz/½ cup stoned (pitted) medjool dates

1.5ml/¼ tsp pink or sea salt

25g/1 oz/¼ cup desiccated raw (dry unsweetened macaroon-cut shredded) coconut

For the filling

140g/5oz fresh rocket (arugula) leaves

350g/12oz/3 cups unroasted cashew nut pieces, soaked overnight

Juice of 4 lemons

175ml/6fl oz/¾ cup clear honey

160ml/5½fl oz/generous ⅔ cup coconut oil, warmed to liquid, plus extra for greasing

A little water, to blend

For the topping

75g/3oz/½ cup stoned (pitted) medjool dates

140g/5oz fresh rocket (arugula), plus some extra leaves to decorate

Edible flowers, to decorate

1 Grease a 23cm/9in springform tin (pan).

2 In a food processor or blender on a low setting, process the walnut pieces, macadamia nuts, dates and salt until they are crumb consistency, then add the coconut and mix together with a spatula. Transfer to the springform tin and press down with a spoon to form an even layer.

3 Make the filling by blending all of the ingredients except the water on medium. Add a little water if needed to help make a creamy consistency, but use as little water as possible. As you blend, intermittently use a spatula to scrape the sides, and increase the power until it's a smooth and creamy consistency, but still as thick as possible.

4 Transfer the filling to the tin, and spread across the base with a spatula. Put it in the freezer for 1–2 hours, to become firm.

5 Start preparing the topping by soaking the dates in just enough cold water to cover, and set aside until the filling in the freezer has set. When ready to continue, blend the dates and rocket with enough of the soaking water to allow them to combine to a paste. Pour the topping over the filling, and return to the freezer for about 4–5 hours, until everything has set.

6 Allow to come up to room temperature, for about half an hour before serving, and decorate with extra rocket leaves and flower sprigs.

Pumpkin Ginger Cheesecake

More of a mousse cake than a cheesecake to be honest, this paleo, vegan and nut-free recipe is easy for everyone to enjoy.

Cooked pumpkin purée is whipped with coconut cream, silken tofu and ginger to make a light filling. My inspiration was Japan, bringing a macrobiotic feeling to this recipe. The pumpkin filling is set on top of a delicious sunflower and ginger crust, making this dairy-free cheesecake also nut-free, which is pretty rare for a cheesecake recipe. It's lighter than most cheesecakes, which makes it a good choice to serve at the end of a special dinner party.

I've written it for canned pumpkin purée, so it's more accessible, but if you have the time, please make your own by baking a pumpkin slowly in an oven set on a low heat. This brings out the nuanced flavours better than any canned pumpkin ever, um, can. The final dessert will be perfectly lovely whichever kind of pumpkin purée you make it with, but it feels negligent not to give you a nudge towards trying it with home-made purée.

1 Grease a 23cm/9in springform cake tin (pan) with coconut oil and line with baking parchment. Preheat the oven to 180°C/350°F/Gas 4.

2 Make the filling first by blending all of the filling ingredients (except the pumpkin) in a blender until totally combined. Set aside to gel while you make the base.

3 Grind the sunflower seeds in a blender or food processor on the highest speed. Add the other base ingredients and continue to process at a low to medium speed until combined to form crumbs. Press the crumbs into the bottom of the tin, making sure it is an even base.

4 Pour the filling on top of the base, and bake for 45–50 minutes, until it's golden and the edges are visibly higher than the centre.

5 Cool on a rack, then chill overnight in the refrigerator. Decorate with strips of raw pumpkin (I use a vegetable peeler) and use a wet knife to cut into clean slices.

MAKES ONE 23CM/9IN CHEESECAKE, SERVES 8–10

For the base

- 140g/5oz/1 cup sunflower seeds
- 5 medjool dates, stoned (pitted)
- 45ml/3 tbsp coconut oil, plus extra for greasing
- 5ml/1 tsp ground ginger

For the filling

- 425g/15oz pumpkin purée, canned or home-cooked
- 120ml/4fl oz/½ cup canned coconut cream, pre-blended, at room temperature
- 350g/12oz soft silken tofu, drained
- 70g/2½oz/⅓ cup maple sugar or coconut sugar
- 30ml/2 tbsp coconut oil, melted
- 30ml/2 tbsp arrowroot
- 1 ripe banana, mashed
- Juice and zest of ½ orange
- 2cm/¾in piece fresh ginger root, finely grated
- 5ml/1 tsp ground ginger
- 1.5ml/¼ tsp pink or sea salt
- Wedge of pumpkin, peeled and pared into strips, to decorate

Purple Prince Cheesecake

Made from purple cabbage, and named after Prince. Because someone had to do it!

This vibrant cheesecake is made with purple cabbage that's blended with tofu, cinnamon and maple syrup on a cauliflower base. Yes – it's a dessert made from purple cabbage and cauliflower. This is the definition of a show-stopping vegan cheesecake, fit for Prince... Don't care where we go, don't care what we do... let's party like it's 1999. Perhaps the only way to go with this is all-out, wearing matching linens, flowers and accessories. While you're at it, light the sparklers too, and of course – make sure you play Purple Rain loud when you serve it.

    GF

MAKES ONE 25CM/10IN CHEESECAKE, SERVES 10

¼ of a head of small purple cabbage

25g/1oz/¼ cup currants

50ml/2fl oz/¼ cup balsamic vinegar

50ml/2fl oz/¼ cup olive oil

2.5ml/½ tsp ground nutmeg

15ml/1 tbsp ground cinnamon

150ml/5fl oz/⅔ cup maple syrup or coconut syrup, plus 50ml/2fl oz/¼ cup

450g/1lb firm silken tofu (Japanese-style)

2.5ml/½ tsp pink or sea salt

2.5ml/½ tsp vanilla extract

30ml/2 tbsp arrowroot

For the base

45ml/3 tbsp ground flax seeds

90ml/3fl oz/6 tbsp water

450g/1lb cauliflower

50g/2oz/½ cup buckwheat flour

5ml/1 tsp vanilla extract

1 Preheat the oven to 200°C/400°F/Gas 6. Line the bottom of a 25cm/10in springform cake tin (pan) with baking parchment.

2 Cut the core out of the purple cabbage, and place in a heat-resistant bowl or casserole dish. Add the currants, balsamic vinegar, olive oil and nutmeg, and 10ml/2 tsp of the cinnamon, and cover tightly with foil, or with a lid if you have one that fits. Set aside.

3 To make the base, in a bowl or cup mix the ground flax seeds and the water, and set aside to thicken. Grate the cauliflower using a box grater or in a food processor so it resembles rice. Tip the grated cauliflower into a clean dish cloth, and squeeze to remove any excess liquid.

4 In a mixing bowl, mix the grated cauliflower with the flax seed mixture, then add the buckwheat flour and vanilla. Press the mixture into the tin, making sure that it's even and tightly packed.

5 Bake the cauliflower base and the purple cabbage mixture simultaneously for 20–25 minutes, until the surface of the cauliflower base is lightly golden brown.

6 Remove both from the oven. Uncover the purple cabbage to baste it in the liquid then re-cover and return it to the oven for a further 10 minutes.

(continued overleaf)

7 Unclip the springform tin (pan) and put a chopping board on top of it, then carefully turn upside down, to flip the baked cauliflower base. Slide the metal plate of the tin away and peel off the parchment to expose the unbaked base. Put the parchment back on the pan bottom, and replace the cauliflower base with the unbaked side upwards. Reassemble the springform and return to the oven for 10 minutes until the top is light golden brown.

8 Remove both the cauliflower and the cabbage from the oven. Allow the cauliflower to cool in the tin, set on a rack, and let the cabbage cool, still covered and in the liquid.

9 When cool enough to handle, shred half of the cooked cabbage for the decorative topping. In a bowl, mix the cooking liquid with the extra 5ml/1 tsp ground cinnamon and the 50ml/2fl oz/¼ cup maple syrup, and fold in the shredded cabbage. Pop into the fridge to marinade.

10 Roughly chop the rest of the purple cabbage, and add to a blender along with the 150ml/5fl oz/²/₃ cup of syrup, the tofu, salt, vanilla extract and arrowroot. Blend until smooth and creamy, scraping the sides down now and then with a spatula.

11 Spoon the tofu mixture over the cauliflower base in the springform tin, and bake for 25 minutes.

12 Cool in the pan on a cooling rack, then chill in the refrigerator until completely firm, for about 2 hours, or overnight. When you are ready to serve, arrange the shredded cabbage decoratively on top.

13 Serve at room temperature, pouring over the marinade to drench each slice of the cheesecake.

Little Cakes

Little cakes are big in impact. They bring pleasure to an otherwise average day, offering bite-sized treats to instantly lift hearts and spirits. They make entertaining a little easier, whether that's time out with friends, or time in with your nearest and dearest. It's the little things in life that count.

So I take this not-so-small task seriously, selecting the perfect vegetable for the little cakes you'll be baking. Take Maple Mushroom Cupcakes, a buttery cupcake with as many kinds of mushroom on top that you care to forage for. There are the oh-so-fashionable ingredients all combined together in Chocolate Avocado Cauliflower Cupcakes. There are gorgeous floral, herbal notes to be found in squishy little moss-green cupcakes topped with lavender-hued frosting, and in the rose-infused brownies. You might be tempted by the luxurious-sounding Waldorf muffins (made with Waldorf salad), courgette financiers and velvety artichoke heart cakes, or artisanal Brooklyn muffins where buckwheat and blackberries are the stage-set for green beans. Explore new horizons with exotic creations such as Lotus Root Wrapper Cakes, or keep it super-sweet and super-simple with cakes (and blondies) made from pumpkin, sweet potato, and beetroot. And – not such a little consideration – all these baked treats are deceptively healthy, even the delicious golden donuts!

Maple Mushroom Cupcakes

Mushrooms, of course, aren't strictly vegetables but are invited here for their wonderful umami taste, unmistakeable texture and nutritional treasure.

These sweet buttery cakes are complemented by the earthy flavour of mushrooms and black sesame seeds, and are topped with tofu-maple frosting scented with vanilla and lemon.

There are thousands of varieties of edible mushroom to explore. For this recipe, I've stipulated button mushrooms because they're so readily available, and they are going to be chopped up and hidden inside these little cakes. But for the top, feel free to go wild, and display some of the more outlandish varieties, like clusters of beautiful, tiny enoki, or orange chanterelle, flowing maitake, and dark, floppy wood ears.

Little cakes that are perfect for an autumn afternoon, even better if you take them outside for a picnic in the woods...

MAKES 9 CUPCAKES

250g/9oz/2 cups spelt flour or wholemeal (whole-wheat) flour

20ml/4 tsp baking powder

2.5ml/½ tsp ground cardamom

400g/14oz button (white) mushrooms

115g/4oz/½ cup/1 stick unsalted butter, at room temperature

115g/4oz/scant ⅔ cup coconut sugar

2 eggs

120ml/4fl oz/½ cup almond milk

30ml/2 tbsp maple syrup

75g/3oz/½ cup black sesame seeds, plus extra for decorating

2.5ml/½ tsp pink or sea salt

A cluster of small edible mushrooms, for decorating

For the frosting

225g/8oz firm tofu

45ml/3 tbsp maple syrup

30ml/2 tbsp olive oil

Juice of ½ lemon

1.5ml/¼ tsp pink or sea salt

2.5ml/½ tsp vanilla extract

1 Preheat the oven to 180°C/350°F/Gas 4. Line a standard small non-stick cupcake tin (pan) with 9 paper cases.

2 Make the frosting by blending all of the ingredients on high until very smooth and creamy. Scrape the sides of the blender to make sure it's all combined, and then set aside.

3 Sift the flour, baking powder and cardamom into a medium bowl, then add the fibre that's left in the sieve or strainer back into the bowl. Stir to incorporate.

4 Wipe clean the mushrooms, then chop them roughly but quite finely, so the pieces are about 5mm/¼in. It doesn't matter if this isn't accurate, but as a guide, aim for about the size of puy lentils.

5 In a large bowl, cream together the butter and coconut sugar with a spoon. Once it's thoroughly mixed, using an electric whisk set to low, add the eggs one at a time, along with roughly a tablespoon of the flour mix for each egg.

6 Turn up the whisk to medium, and beat while you add half of the almond milk. Keep beating while you add half of the remaining flour mixture, and then the rest of the almond milk, and the maple syrup. Add the remaining flour mixture, sesame seeds and salt, and beat to combine. Stir in the chopped mushrooms using a spoon.

7 Spoon the mixture evenly into the cupcake cases and bake for 23–25 minutes. Test by inserting a skewer into the middle of a cupcake; they're ready when the skewer comes out clean. Then leave to cool for about 10 minutes.

8 Remove the cupcakes carefully, and leave on a rack to cool completely. When they're cool, spread the tops with the frosting, and sprinkle with sesame seeds and small mushrooms to decorate.

Chocolate Avocado Cauliflower Cupcakes

These light kid-friendly cauliflower cupcakes are topped with chocolate avocado frosting and scattered with petit pois to decorate, instead of sugar sprinkles.

The basis for this cupcake batter is cauliflower that's been grated or riced. The simple blend of flours retains the moisture of the cauliflower, but adds a lightness to it. It's this combination that makes these little cakes so appealing to little people – because they're light.

Children invariably like petit pois, so I serve these cupcakes with tiny green spheres in the creamy chocolate-avocado frosting. I hope you get some giggles, as well as happy chocolate-y faces grinning back at you after they've all been eaten up! Alternatively why not sprinkle with alfalfa sprouts for a very '70s boho vibe.

MAKES 12 CUPCAKES

- 175g/6oz/1½ cups raw cauliflower florets
- Zest and juice of ½ lemon
- 50ml/2fl oz/¼ cup cold tea, any variety
- 50g/2oz/½ cup brown rice flour
- 30g/1oz/¼ cup oat flour
- 30g/1oz/¼ cup potato starch
- 30g/1oz/¼ cup raw cacao powder
- 5ml/1 tsp bicarbonate of soda (baking soda)
- 1.5ml/¼ tsp pink or sea salt
- 2 eggs

- 120ml/4fl oz/½ cup olive oil
- 100g/3¾oz/½ cup coconut sugar
- 50g/2oz/½ cup frozen petit pois, to decorate
- Sprigs of peashoots, alfalfa sprouts or microherbs, to decorate

For the frosting

- 2 ripe avocados
- 50ml/2fl oz/¼ cup maple syrup
- 1.5ml/¼ tsp pink or sea salt

(continued overleaf)

1 Preheat the oven to 180°C/350°F/Gas 4. Line a medium cupcake tin (pan) with 12 paper cases.

2 Using the coarse side of a box grater, shred the cauliflower into a bowl. Add the lemon zest and juice to the cauliflower and mix in the cold tea, then set aside to marinate while you carry out the next steps.

3 Sift the flours, cacao, bicarbonate of soda and pink salt into a medium bowl.

4 In a large bowl, beat the eggs, olive oil and coconut sugar together with an electric whisk set to medium. When combined, keep beating on medium and add the flour mixture roughly 50g/2oz/½ cup at a time until it's all combined to form a cohesive batter. Fold in the cauliflower mixture along with its liquid.

5 Spoon the batter in equal amounts into the cupcake cases, and bake in the oven for about 23–25 minutes. The cupcakes will be ready when a skewer inserted into the middle comes out clean and free from crumbs. Leave them to cool in the tin for about 10 minutes, and then remove to completely cool on a cooling rack.

6 While the cupcakes are baking, make the frosting by mashing the avocados in a bowl using a fork. Add the maple syrup and salt and keep combining until it is a very smooth and creamy frosting. Alternatively, mix all the frosting ingredients in a food processor or blender until smooth. Chill the frosting in the refrigerator so that it firms up as the cakes cool.

7 Bring 50ml/2fl oz/¼ cup water to the boil in a small pan, and add the frozen petit pois. Simmer for about 6 minutes covered, then drain and set them aside to cool.

8 When the cakes are cool and you're ready to serve, spread or pipe the frosting on top, and decorate with the petit pois and sprigs of herb. The cupcakes will stay fresh at room temperature for 2 days if unfrosted, but need to be eaten within a few hours once the avocado frosting is on top.

Lavender Spinach Cupcakes

Using almond flour and aquafaba, these little almond cupcakes are a pretty mossy green colour, with a subtle herbal note and a lovely purple blueberry-lavender frosting.

These are squishy super-moist cupcakes, perfect for grown-ups and children alike. The recipe will work without the guar gum if you don't have that ingredient, but it's definitely better if you can find some, as it ensures the non-wheat flours bind well in the absence of eggs. The olive oil and cider vinegar combination is a tried and tested fusion and equally it's a fantastic vegan way to replace the binding power of eggs.

You don't have to be vegan to eat these, of course, but it's a lovely way to balance out our reliance on animal-based foods, and to explore a more flexible approach to how we label ourselves, and our diets. Just like vegetable cakes – we are opening our minds to other possibilities.

All that inside each tiny cupcake!

DF VG SF GF

MAKES 12 CUPCAKES

- 280g/10oz/roughly 2 bags baby spinach leaves
- 100g/3¾oz/1 cup almond flour
- 100g/3¾oz/1 cup oat flour
- 115g/4oz/scant ⅔ cup coconut sugar
- 20ml/4 tsp bicarbonate of soda (baking soda)
- 10ml/2 tsp guar gum
- 2.5ml/½ tsp pink or sea salt
- 100ml/3½fl oz/scant ½ cup aquafaba i.e. the liquid from canned chickpeas
- 120ml/4fl oz/½ cup olive oil
- 60ml/4 tbsp apple cider vinegar
- 10ml/2 tsp almond extract
- Lavender flowers, to decorate

For the frosting

- 100g/3¾oz/¾ cup unroasted cashew nuts, soaked overnight
- 50ml/2fl oz/¼ cup maple syrup
- 40g/1½oz/¼ cup frozen blueberries
- 1 drop lavender essential oil
- 1.5ml/¼ tsp pink or sea salt
- 60ml/4 tbsp coconut oil, melted
- 15–30ml/1–2 tbsp warm water, if necessary

(continued overleaf)

1 Place the spinach into a lidded pan, add about 30ml/
2 tbsp of water and heat over a low heat for a few minutes,
until the spinach has wilted and reduced to a cooked
mass. Lift out the spinach, discarding any liquid, and set
aside the solid mass in a bowl to cool. It will measure
about 75g/2½oz/⅓ cup.

2 Next, make the frosting. Drain and rinse the cashew
nuts, and transfer to a high-speed blender. Add the maple
syrup, blueberries, lavender oil and salt, and blend with
coconut oil and water, as needed, to help it process.
Transfer to the refrigerator, and leave to set while you
make the cakes.

3 Preheat the oven to 180°C/350°F/Gas 4. Line a medium
12-cup cake tin (pan) with squares of baking parchment or
paper cases.

4 Sift the almond and oat flour, coconut sugar,
bicarbonate of soda, guar gum and salt into a large bowl,
adding back the larger particles after any clusters have
been broken up. Stir together.

5 Blend the cooked spinach with the aquafaba, oil,
vinegar and almond extract in a food processor or blender
on low, steadily turning up the speed over a minute to
make a smooth blended purée. Pour it into the bowl of dry
ingredients. Stir the wet and dry ingredients together.

6 Spoon the batter into the cases and bake for about
18–20 minutes. Leave to cool in the tin for about 5 minutes,
and then remove the cakes and allow to cool completely
on a wire rack. Take the frosting out of the fridge.

7 Once the cakes have cooled, spread the tops with the
lavender frosting, then chill until it sets. Decorate the cakes
with lavender flowers.

COOK'S TIPS
If it's a cold day, the coconut oil may solidify in the blender
while you're trying to make the frosting, in which case, run
the outside of the container under hot water, and blend.

Due to their delicate squishy nature, these little cakes
must be eaten on the day they're baked, and frosted soon
before serving. They're worth it, as they're so moist.

Try adding 10ml/2 tsp matcha tea powder to impart a
subtle, slightly bitter note and to boost the green colour.

Waldorf Muffins

Like a Waldorf salad, but in a cake! Made with celery, apples, lettuce and walnuts, these are simple and quick to whip up. They're on the sweeter side of life.

Waldorf Salad is named after the hotel in New York, a grand Victorian edifice that opened on Fifth Avenue in 1893. It was built by the Astor family, who hailed from the town of Waldorf, in Germany.

The maître d'hotel was Oscar Tschirky, and in 1893 he invented the salad for a charity ball, after which the recipe became an enduring classic of the era. Over the years, there have been many tweaks and changes, as different ingredients have come in and out of vogue. Endless permutations have graced tables, all presented as Waldorf Salad, so it seems perfectly acceptable to recreate it as a muffin, and a vegan one at that!

Apple sauce is the secret binding ingredient – it's a double-action winner, replacing the need for both eggs and sugar. There's a touch of coconut sugar to bump up the sweetness, but overall, the apple sauce plays a big role in these little muffins.

In the States, apple sauce is available in every shop and is a pantry staple. To make your own, simply cook peeled and cored apples with a little water until soft, say 10 minutes, then purée or press through a sieve. It's an invaluable ingredient to keep in the fridge.

MAKES 12 MUFFINS

300g/11oz/2½ cups wholemeal (whole-wheat) flour

70g/2½oz/⅓ cup coconut sugar

10ml/2 tsp baking powder

10ml/2 tsp ground cinnamon

1.5ml/¼ tsp pink or sea salt

4 large and 12 baby lettuce leaves

25cm/10in stick of celery

50g/2oz/½ cup walnut pieces

375g/13oz/1½ cups apple sauce

120ml/4fl oz/½ cup olive oil

12 apple pieces

30ml/2 tbsp canned coconut cream to drizzle, optional

1 Preheat the oven to 180°C/350°F/Gas 4. Place 12 paper cases into a muffin tin (pan).

2 Stir the flour, coconut sugar, baking powder, cinnamon and salt together in a bowl.

3 Tear the large lettuce leaves. Chop the celery into pieces, roughly 8cm/3in.

4 Place the celery, torn lettuce and walnuts in a blender with the apple sauce and olive oil and blend on low, raising the speed to medium over about 30 seconds. It's ready when you can still see chunks of vegetables, but it's more like a chunky smoothie.

5 Pour the smoothie into the dry ingredients, and stir to combine. Fill the muffin cases until nearly level, and top with a piece of apple and a small lettuce leaf on each.

6 Put into the oven and bake for 30 minutes, until a toothpick inserted into the middle comes out clean. Leave to cool in the baking tin. If you like, drizzle over a little coconut cream for contrast and additional sweetness.

COOK'S TIPS

To continue the Waldorf theme, add 50g/2oz/½ cup sultanas (golden raisins) to the dry ingredients. I also sometimes add a little raw cacao powder.

For another frosting idea, combine one ripe avocado with one medjool date, blending well to create a paste. Spread on top of the muffins and serve immediately.

Velvet Artichoke Hearts

Delicate, tender artichoke hearts nestle inside honey and olive oil cakes. Sweet and moist, these special little muffins are velvety in texture, due to the almond flour.

Artichokes are simply flower buds from the artichoke plant, which I've grown in my garden. They're huge spiky thistles that grow in one round clump, with dusty green misty leaves that are serrated like a knife and develop from a giant base to delicate and feather-like top. Each plant needs a lot of space and can grow a lot of buds. Technically speaking, they're not vegetables as such – they're flower buds – but they're eaten like vegetables, usually as a part of an antipasto, in green salads, or on top of pizzas. And they are surprisingly good in a sweet cake.

Artichokes taste like nothing else – there's a dominant flavour note in them that doesn't resemble any other food. I think they are irresistible, whether they're freshly steamed, marinated or simply taken ready-cooked from a can.

For this recipe, you can steam fresh baby artichokes, or use canned or marinated artichoke hearts out of a jar. They'll all make wonderful, very special little cakes that will be remembered for a long time. You could bake these in mini Panettone cups instead of muffin tins; they have straight sides and a sophisticated look.

MAKES 12 MUFFINS

3 boiled and choked canned globe artichoke hearts, quartered (roughly 200g/7oz/half a can, drained well), or 12 tiny fresh baby artichokes

200g/7oz/1¾ cup spelt flour

50g/2oz/½ cup ground almonds

10ml/2 tsp baking powder

1.5ml/¼ tsp pink or sea salt

2 eggs

250ml/8fl oz/generous 1 cup clear honey

175ml/6fl oz/¾ cup olive oil

120ml/4fl oz/½ cup milk

5ml/1 tsp vanilla extract

1 Preheat the oven to 180°C/350°F/Gas 4. Shape 12 squares of baking parchment around a small cylinder, such as a baking powder container, and place in a 12-cup muffin tin (pan).

2 Mix together the flour, almonds, baking powder and salt in a bowl.

3 Beat the eggs in a large mixing bowl with an electric whisk set to medium for about a minute.

4 Add the honey, oil, milk and vanilla, and continue beating for about a minute until combined.

5 Add the dry mixture to the wet ingredients, whisking until they're roughly combined.

6 Using a large tablespoon, add enough batter so each parchment case is three-quarters full. Place one artichoke quarter in each, then transfer enough of the batter to nearly immerse the hearts and to fill the case until it's level. Ideally it's nice to have a little bit of artichoke visible in the muffin, but if they're entirely immersed, that's okay.

7 Bake in the middle of the oven for 20–22 minutes, until the tops are puffy and golden brown.

8 Allow to cool, and either eat immediately or store in an airtight container. However they'll become even better the day after they're baked, when the olive oil has thoroughly moistened the cake throughout.

COOK'S TIPS

The easiest way to make these is with canned hearts, but if you do find little baby artichokes in the market, they are lovely as you can eat the whole thing, and they look so sweet peeping up out of the sponge. Just lightly boil or steam them before using in the recipe. If they are very tiny you could use one per cake, or quarter them if larger.

Choose dark honey if you like, for a more pronounced honey flavour.

Brooklyn Scones

These rustic scones use buckwheat as an enticing dark setting for vivid green beans and purple blackberries.

I wrote this recipe when I was still living in a brownstone Victorian house in Bushwick, a leafy neighbourhood in Brooklyn known for its high concentration of artistic people and for its wonderful multi-cultural culinary culture. Many of the independent cafés put a creative spin on classic European favourites, Don't be fooled – the word 'scone' means something completely different in American English than in British English. Both are perfectly acceptable, but don't expect a British scone from this recipe; it's more like a British rock cake, but with a triangle shape instead of a rocky blob shape.

The buckwheat flour makes for dark scones, which become even darker from crushed blackberries that provide bursts of purple. Dotted with dark green beans, these have an artisan-urban sophistication that epitomises Brooklyn. And the almond flour and coconut cream give a super-rich and velvety texture. They're unusual in the best way. I like to serve them with whipped coconut cream.

MAKES 8 LARGE OR 12 SMALL SLICES

100g/3¾oz/¾ cup green beans

15ml/1 tbsp flaxseed meal

200g/7oz/2 cups ground almonds

200g/7oz/1¾ cups buckwheat flour, plus extra for dusting

120g/4oz/1 cup potato starch

15ml/1 tbsp baking powder

2.5ml/½ tsp pink or sea salt, plus extra for sprinkling

400ml/14fl oz can of coconut cream, chilled (see step 5)

60ml/4 tbsp maple syrup

5ml/1 tsp vanilla extract

75g/3oz/½ cup blackberries

1 Top and tail the green beans. Steam the beans in a steamer basket for about 5 minutes, then set aside to cool. Alternatively, boil for 3 minutes, and plunge in cold water.

2 Preheat the oven to 220°C/425°F/Gas 7. Lightly dust a baking tray with flour.

3 Mix the flaxseed meal with 45ml/3 tbsp warm water, and leave to become a gel.

4 Combine the ground almonds, buckwheat flour, potato starch, baking powder and salt in a large mixing bowl using a whisk.

5 Drain off the liquid from the refrigerated can of coconut cream, then measure out 175ml/6fl oz/1 cup of the solid cream (this is most of the can) into a bowl and add the maple syrup and vanilla. Mix well, using your hands and palms to knead together.

6 On a lightly floured surface form the dough roughly into a circle. Crush the blackberries and gently knead them and the green beans into the dough, maintaining the circular shape. Cut the dough into 8 triangles.

7 Sprinkle with some extra salt and bake for about 25 minutes, until they are a lovely golden brown.

8 Allow to cool for 3 minutes in the baking tray, then transfer to a wire rack to cool completely, This recipe makes 8 USA-sized scones or 12 UK-sized ones.

Lotus Root Wrapper Cakes

It all started with the look. Who can resist ordering summer spring rolls at a Vietnamese restaurant simply to see the transparent wrappers glowing with bright colours inside.

Fast forward to now, and I've perfected the sweetest vegetable fusion-dessert, scented with cinnamon and mint, with a dipping sauce that's a sensuous drop of South-East Asia.

I love the way the rice wrappers reveal the lotus root with a tantalising semi-transparent glimpse, suggesting the unique crunch of their cloud-like shape, all underscored with a burst of pomegranate juice and tang of shiso leaf.

It's a two-part recipe; first prepare the wrapper cakes, including the pre-cake preparation of each of the filling ingredients, and secondly, make the sesame-coconut dipping sauce to serve on the side.

This is a lovely sweet to make with company, so find a child or adult friend to help. Each of the ingredient preparation stages takes a minute, so allow a relaxed amount of time to enjoy the visual creativity. Plan ahead for the marinating, too.

NF   DF   SF   GF

MAKES 12 WRAPPERS

12 Vietnamese round rice paper wrappers

50g/2oz rice vermicelli

30ml/2 tbsp ground cinnamon

15ml/1 tbsp ground turmeric

60ml/4 tbsp rice vinegar

200g/7oz lotus roots, cooked and sliced

12 shiso leaves

seeds of 1 pomegranate

Other filling ingredients of your choice: carrots, sprigs of fresh mint, mizuna leaves, mung or other mild bean sprouts, daikon shreds, cucumber ribbons, bell pepper strips, chopped dried apricot, grated turmeric, fresh nectarine wedges

3 fresh limes, cut into wedges, to serve

For the dipping sauce

60ml/4 tbsp sesame oil

60ml/4 tbsp clear honey

250ml/8fl oz/1 cup coconut milk, warmed

(continued overleaf)

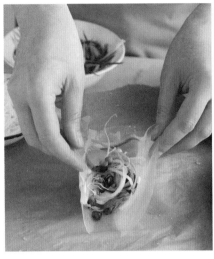  

1 Fill a deep heatproof bowl with boiling water, and immerse the rice vermicelli, being careful not to break too many of them. Using tongs, move the vermicelli around every minute until they are totally soft and cooked. Drain the noodles, and set aside to cool.

2 Put the ground cinnamon and turmeric into a medium lidded container, and add the rice vinegar and cover. Shake vigorously to combine, then remove the lid and add the slices of lotus root. Set aside to marinate for at least 20 minutes, or overnight.

3 Prepare the various ingredients for filling the wrappers, storing them in a damp paper towel or dish cloth as you work. Peel the carrots and daikon, top and tail them, and carefully cut them into thin long strips, or into ribbons using a vegetable peeler. De-seed bell peppers and cut into thin strips. Cut cucumber or courgette into thin julienne-style strips. Slice nectarines into small wedges and chop up a few dried apricots for bites of sweetness.

4 When you're ready to compile the wrapper cakes, fill a large bowl with warm water. Carefully immerse one of the rice paper wrappers in the water for about a minute, until it's soft and totally flexible. You may need to start with one end, and move it through the water slowly, unless you have a bowl that's large enough for the entire wrapper to fit into.

5 When the rice paper is soft and flexible, carefully lay it on to a sheet of baking parchment. Place a lotus root slice, a shiso leaf, a few pomegranate seeds, and a little of all your chosen ingredients into the centre of each wrapper.

6 Gather up the edges of the wrapper around the filling and gently twist the edges to secure. Place the roll on to a serving platter. Repeat this process for all 12 rolls.

7 To make the dipping sauce, mix the sesame oil and honey into the warm coconut milk.

8 Serve with lime wedges and a dish of dipping sauce.

COOK'S TIPS
These are delicious with an optional layer of peanut butter inside the wrapper, or as an addition to the dipping sauce, if peanuts are part of your diet. The recipe can be gluten-free if you check the rice wrappers and vermicelli.

If you are de-seeding a fresh pomegranate, fill a large bowl with cold water. Using a sharp knife, cut the top off the pomegranate. Immerse the pomegranate in the water, then start to break it open and peel it with your fingers. Allow the seeds and the outer skin and membranes to come apart. When the fruit has been totally taken apart, skim all of the inedible parts from the surface of the water, and then drain the water to leave the clean seeds in the bowl ready to use.

Sweet Potato Fudge Blondies

Moist enough to eat with a spoon, and fudgy, with a rich colour and delicate spice – these get the star prize for being super-sweet and super-simple.

These are reminiscent, in their use of spices, to the classic American sweet potatoes that are served at Thanksgiving. The sunflower seed butter is also a traditional American ingredient, although it's become more neglected over the years as peanut and almond butters have come to the fore. The humble sunflower is the rich gold of the East Coast in my opinion, with similar flavour notes to the other members of the sunflower family we eat, including artichokes, lettuce and sunchokes.

There's no other oil or fat in this recipe; it's enough as it is, combined with the natural moistness of the steamed sweet potatoes. That's what makes this such a simple, effective recipe to whip up on a whim, without needing a lot of time or effort for preparation. Also, you can simplify the ingredients by replacing the coconut flour with oat flour if you're able.

Either way, these are lovely squishy cakes, best eaten on the day of baking, after they've cooled.

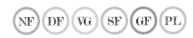

MAKES 15 BLONDIES

- 300g/11oz/roughly 2 large sweet potatoes, steamed, cooled and peeled
- 115g/4oz/½ cup sunflower seed butter
- 50g/2oz/½ cup coconut flour
- 120g/4¼oz/⅔ cup coconut sugar
- 5ml/1 tsp ground cinnamon, plus extra for dusting
- 5ml/1 tsp ground cardamom
- 5ml/1 tsp vanilla extract
- 5ml/1 tsp baking powder
- 1.5ml/¼ tsp pink or sea salt

1 Preheat the oven to 180°C/350°F/Gas 4. Line a 20cm/8in square baking tin (pan) with baking parchment.

2 Mash the sweet potatoes in the pan with a potato masher or fork until smooth.

3 Add all of the other ingredients to a bowl with the mashed sweet potato, and combine using a fork.

4 Transfer the mixture to the prepared baking tin, then level and smooth the top.

5 Bake for 30 minutes until a crust can be seen on top, and the sides start to pull away from the tin.

6 Allow to cool in the tin, then remove and cut into 5cm/2in squares. Dust with extra cinnamon and serve.

COOK'S TIPS
If you are able to eat oats, you can substitute coconut flour with rolled oats that have been blitzed in a food processor, or with oat flour.

If preferred, substitute the sunflower seed butter with tahini or almond butter.

Beetroot Rose Chocolate Brownies

This flourless, eggless recipe makes the most of the versatile beet as the base ingredient, transformed during baking into a (nearly) traditional rich-tasting brownie.

The wonderful consistency of puréed beetroot forms the substance of this brownie, while the binding power of chickpea water is a vehicle for the chocolate and rose flavours to be delivered.

Confronting expectations, this is a gentle dessert cake that's as easy on the tongue as it is on the eye. It also provides a key to considering vegetable dyes for decoration, with the simple technique for dying coconut equally good when tried with other vegetable dyes, from purple cabbage to onion skins.

Essential oils vary considerably in strength. With a high-quality essential oil, one drop will be plenty.

Serve with rosehip tea to complement the colour as much as the robust flavours.

NF DF VG SF GF

MAKES 20 BROWNIES

500g/1¼ lb whole beetroots (beets)

100ml/3½fl oz/scant ½ cup coconut oil

50ml/2fl oz/¼ cup maple syrup

200g/7oz dark chocolate, 100% cocoa solids, chopped

100ml/3½fl oz/scant ½ cup aquafaba i.e. the liquid from canned chickpeas

100g/3¾ oz/½ cup coconut sugar

up to 5ml/1 tsp rose otto (damask) essential oil

Pinch of pink or sea salt

80g/3¼ oz cornflour (cornstarch)

5ml/1 tsp baking powder

25g/1oz desiccated raw (dry unsweetened macaroon-cut shredded) coconut

(continued overleaf)

1 Preheat the oven to 200°C/400°F/Gas 6 and grease and line a 20 x 30cm/8 x 12in baking tin (pan). Place the beetroots in a pan of boiling water and bring back to the boil. Simmer for 20 minutes until soft.

2 Drain, reserving a small glass of the liquid. Allow the beetroots to cool, then peel. Liquidise in a blender until a purée-like consistency, then transfer the beetroot pulp to a large mixing bowl.

3 Mix the oil, syrup and chocolate with the beetroot and stir thoroughly until combined.

4 In a separate bowl, whisk the aquafaba with an electric whisk for 4 minutes until thick and glossy. Whisk in the sugar for 30 seconds, then fold the mixture into the beetroot. Add the rose oil (just a drop or two is needed if you are using the purest oil) and salt, then mix in the cornflour and baking powder.

5 Pour the batter into the prepared tin and bake for 15 minutes, or until set on top. Turn the oven down to 180°C/350°F/Gas 4 and cook for a further 15 minutes. Allow to cool completely.

6 In the meantime, scatter half of the desiccated coconut on another baking tin lined with baking parchment and sprinkle over 10ml/2 tsp of the reserved beetroot cooking water. Mix briefly then turn the oven down to 100°C/200°F/Gas ¼ and bake for 5 minutes.

7 Cut the brownie into squares and sprinkle with the dyed purply-pink coconut and the remaining white desiccated coconut. Serve.

Pumpkin Coffee Blondie Brownies

Are they blondies if they're brown? Are they brownies if they don't contain chocolate? Perhaps they should be Brownie Blondies... but who cares when they taste this good!

These blondie brownies contain large amounts of sophistication for such little cakes, The coffee brings depth to match the darkness of the buckwheat, and classic pumpkin spicing adds autumnal tones.

It's possible to skip a pumpkin step by using canned pumpkin, but how much time does it take to make pumpkin purée from scratch, and how much better does it taste? It's worth the effort if you're able to buy fresh pumpkin instead. (Perhaps the exception would be the 'Midnight' Blondie Brownie, which is the version that's rustled up after dark using the can of pumpkin from the back of your cupboard... The moonbeams you stir into the batter at that time of night brighten any flavour notes absent from not roasting fresh pumpkin.)

This recipe makes enough blondie brownies for three midnight picnics for two people.

1 Preheat the oven to 180°C/350°F/Gas 4 and grease and line a 20 x 30cm/8 x 12in baking tin (pan).

2 Place the pumpkin flesh on a baking sheet and roast for 20 minutes. Blend the pumpkin in a food processor then transfer to a large mixing bowl. Mix in the oil, maple syrup, all of the spices and the espresso.

3 In a separate mixing bowl, whisk the aquafaba with an electric whisk for 4 minutes, or until thick and glossy. Mix it into the pumpkin mixture and then gently fold in the buckwheat flour.

4 Transfer the batter into the prepared tin and sprinkle with pumpkin seeds. Bake for 40 minutes, or until set on top. Allow to cool completely. Cut the brownie into slices.

NF DF VG SF GF PL

MAKES 12 SLICES

600g/1lb 6oz pumpkin flesh, chopped

100ml/3½fl oz/scant ½ cup pumpkin seed oil, plus extra for greasing

100ml/3½fl oz/scant ½ cup maple syrup

¼ whole nutmeg, freshly grated

5ml/1 tsp ground cinnamon

1.5ml/¼ tsp ground ginger

Pinch of ground cloves

60ml/4 tbsp/2 shots of espresso coffee

60ml/4 tbsp aquafaba i.e. the liquid from canned chickpeas

125g/4½oz/generous 1 cup buckwheat flour

50g/2oz pumpkin seeds, to sprinkle

Courgette Financiers

Financiers are so-named, it is thought, for the shape of their traditional rectangular tin, which resembles a bar of gold, or because it suits the copious rich ingredients they contain.

MAKES 10 CAKES

½ courgette (zucchini)

25g/1oz pistachio nuts

80g/3¼oz/⅓ cup/¾ stick unsalted butter, plus extra for greasing

80g/3¼oz/scant ¾ cup plain (all-purpose) flour

80g/3¼oz ground almonds

5ml/1 tsp baking powder

Pinch of pink or sea salt

3 egg whites

30ml/2 tbsp maple syrup

Edible dried rose petals

1 Preheat the oven to 200°C/400°F/Gas 6 and grease 10 small individual loaf tins (pans), or special financier tins if you can find them.

2 Prepare the toppings by peeling thin ribbons of courgette using a vegetable peeler, and lightly crushing the pistachio nuts (in a pestle or mortar or with the back of a knife; it's nice to keep a few decorative larger pieces).

2 Melt the butter in a small pan over a medium heat then simmer for 3 minutes or until it starts to brown. Take the pan off the heat.

3 Combine all the dry ingredients in a bowl, then add the egg whites and syrup. Stir thoroughly until you have a thick batter. Mix in the brown butter.

4 Fill the prepared tins with equal amounts of the batter and top with the courgette strips, pistachio nuts and rose petals. Bake for 15 minutes.

COOK'S TIP

Place the ribboned courgette in a bowl of water to keep fresh whilst you prepare the cake batter.

... and yet another theory is that they are called this because Parisian stockbrokers tucked them into their jacket pockets! I'm no stranger to vegan cakes, but the financier is one cake that demands oodles of brown butter. Add to that a hefty serving of ground almonds and pistachios and you have the basis for luxuriant little tea cakes. These are topped with curls of courgette, adding twists of glamour to a quietly confident and (underneath the vegetable and rose petal topping) actually rather old-fashioned recipe. Unexpected at first sight but definitely elegant; if not quite your grandmother's (or stockbroker's) idea of a financier, they are something she'd enjoy nonetheless.

Butternut Squash 'Donuts'

These gorgeous yeasted buns are stuffed with an outrageous chocolate coconut cream, but you can still feel good about indulging in them, because they're baked, not deep-fried.

This is a tale of two languages. Before we even start discussing the secret vegetable in the recipe, we need to decide, are these donuts or doughnuts?

If they're American donuts, please simply make and bake, and serve with coffee.

If they're British doughnuts, you're going to need to fill them to avoid disappointment, as the British version is always filled, unless it's shaped in a ring. This chocolate cream filling is sumptuous, and reminiscent of the Krispy Kreme variety. It does the job fabulously alongside the butternut squash dough, which is made with traditional yeast for an authentic donut/doughnut taste.

As with any butternut squash recipe, your options for cooking it include steaming, boiling, or roasting. Roasting is always the best in terms of caramelising the flavours, and adding sweetness, but it's also slightly more time-consuming. For this reason, I've suggested steaming it, which destroys less of the flavours and nutrients than boiling. Feel free to roast the squash instead if you prefer. However you cook it, and whether these donuts are plain or filled, you're in for a treat.

1 Place the butternut squash pieces in a lidded steamer basket over a large pan of gently boiling water, and steam for 15 minutes, until soft. Drain and allow to cool slightly.

2 In a bowl mash the butternut squash and butter together until smooth, then add the flour and sugar and combine with a spoon. Stir in the yeast, beaten egg and milk. Knead by hand on a surface dusted with flour for 10 minutes, or 5 minutes in a machine with a dough hook. The dough will be soft and loose. Place in a clean bowl and cover with greased clear film or plastic wrap. Leave in a warm place to prove for 45 minutes to 1 hour or until the dough has doubled in size. Grease a flat baking sheet.

3 Turn the dough out on to a liberally floured surface and dust the top of the dough with flour. Flatten slightly with a rolling pin so it is around 5cm/2in thick. With a round cookie cutter, cut out about 10 donuts, re-rolling the leftover batter. Place spaced out on the sheet, cover with a large piece of greased clear film, and leave in a warm place to double in size. This will take 20–30 minutes. Preheat the oven to 190°C/375°F/Gas 5 and bake the donuts for 10 minutes until golden-brown. Allow to cool.

4 In a bowl, whip the cream with an electric whisk for 2 minutes or until thick. In a double-boiler or bowl set over a small pan of simmering water, melt the chocolate (about 45 seconds), then stir into the cream. Transfer the chocolate cream into a piping bag. Make a small incision in each donut, then pipe about 15ml/1 tbsp of cream into the middles. Dust with cinnamon and serve.

MAKES 10 DONUTS/DOUGHNUTS

500g/1¼lb butternut squash, peeled and chopped

30ml/2 tbsp butter, plus extra for greasing

400g/14oz/3½ cups plain (all-purpose) flour, plus extra for dusting

40g/1½oz coconut sugar

7g/¼oz dried fast-action yeast

1 egg, beaten

30ml/2 tbsp full-fat (whole) milk

200ml/7fl oz/scant 1 cup double (heavy) cream

50g/2oz dark chocolate, 100% cocoa solids

Ground cinnamon, for dusting

Sweet Potato Cakes

This is one of my crowd-pleasing family favourites, due to its easy simplicity and potential to involve kids of all ages in its preparation.

These are haystack-like, crispy little cakes. Sweet potatoes come in many varieties, but all work wonderfully in this recipe. For a lighter option, feel free to substitute the ground almonds with wholemeal flour or gluten-free flours such as rice flour, fine cornmeal or potato flour. Simply replace the ground almonds with the same amount of your chosen flour. If you don't serve with yogurt, they are dairy-free.

(SF) (GF) (PL)

MAKES 8

15ml/1 tbsp coconut oil, for greasing

500g/1¼lb sweet potatoes

45ml/3 tbsp ground almonds

2.5ml/½ tsp ground cinnamon, plus extra for sprinkling

1.5ml/¼ tsp ground cardamom

0.7ml/⅛ tsp baking powder

2 eggs, lightly beaten

Greek (US strained plain) yogurt, to serve (optional)

1 Preheat the oven to 220°C/425°F/ Gas 7. Grease a baking sheet with oil and line it with baking parchment.

2 Grate the unpeeled sweet potatoes using a food processor or a box grater, then spread them out on a clean dish towel to absorb any excess juices.

3 Put the grated sweet potatoes in a mixing bowl with the ground almonds, spices and baking powder. Add the eggs and mix to combine, working quickly.

4 Divide the mixture into 8 equal portions and put them on the baking sheet. Flatten each portion so they are round, and about 1cm/½in thick.

5 Bake for 15 minutes on one side, then remove from the oven briefly. Flip each of the cakes over and rotate the baking sheet before returning it to the oven. Bake for 10 minutes more, or until the cakes are crispy and brown.

6 Serve with Greek yogurt to dunk the cakes into, if you like, and sprinkled with cinnamon.

Tarts and Pies

Using vegetables in sweet tarts and pies could be trickier than cakes, because tarts and pies resemble quiches and flans, and you want to give visual cues that let your tastebuds know they're about to be hit with something sweet before you take your first bite.

Red Romanesco Tart does that beautifully, with the raspberry-poached spirals jutting out of the pink fluffy coconut cream, like a little picture of heaven at sunrise. The Parsnip Upside Down Tarte isn't quite as visual as that (what could be as pretty as pink and green clouds?) but it does have the appearance of a sweet cake. I drew inspiration from tarte tatin, but switched apples (or pears) for parsnips. Seriously, this is a great and very grown-up dessert.

The Courgette Rosette Tart is just too curly to possibly be a quiche, with the pretty rosettes preparing the palate for sweetness. It's filled with crème anglaise and has an optional wine glaze. Some recipes like the Broccoli Custard Flan aren't so far away from a quiche in structure, but the custard is sweet instead of being salty and oniony, and the vanilla softens the vegetable in a warm, mellow way.

And then there are the rustic galettes; one with fiddlehead ferns and another with Brussels sprouts on a hazelnut frangipane (which is made with a fair amount of Bourbon whisky!). These might push the boundaries of what is usually expected in a tart but the proof is in the eating – my mission is to be playful, discover new things, and be creative. Enjoy your tart adventure.

Salted Caramel Swiss Chard Pie

This might look like a salad but rest assured, it's very much a pie — and what a pie, with dairy cream mixed with butter and coconut sugar for caramelly gorgeousness.

I could describe this as a caramel tart, with added herbs... or perhaps as a quiche without the egg but with extra toffee. It certainly has the finest, butteriest, crumbliest pastry that's crisp in texture and high on flavour, and even if you need to take a breath before embracing the emerald, you will fall in love with it once tried. A brilliant green whimsical tart infused with salty caramel sweetness.

MAKES ONE 23CM/9IN PIE, SERVES 6–8

100g/3¾oz/1 cup cornflour (cornstarch), plus extra for dusting

100g/3¾oz/1 cup buckwheat flour

250g/9oz/generous 1 cup/2¼ sticks chilled unsalted butter, cubed, plus extra for greasing

1 egg

80g/3oz/⅓ cup generous coconut sugar, plus 15ml/1 tbsp

100ml/3½fl oz/scant ½ cup single (light) cream

Pinch of sea salt

250g/9oz Swiss chard

Edible flowers, to decorate

1 Place the cornflour and buckwheat flour in a bowl and mix to combine. Add 150g/5oz of the butter and rub into the flour mixture with your fingertips until completely integrated. Mix in the egg and 15ml/1 tbsp of the sugar, then stir together to make a sticky dough. Wrap in clear film or plastic wrap and chill for 1 hour.

2 Grease a 23cm/9in fluted, loose-bottomed pie tin (pan). On a clean surface dusted with cornflour, roll out the pastry to a little bigger than the tin. Place the pastry into the tin and chill for 30 minutes. Preheat the oven to 200°C/400°F/Gas 6.

3 Trim around the edge of the tart to neaten, cutting a little higher than the tin. Cover with baking parchment and fill with baking beans and bake blind for 10 minutes. Remove the parchment and beans and cook for a further 5 minutes. Take out of the oven and turn the temperature down to 180°C/350°F/Gas 4.

4 In a small pan, bring the remaining butter and coconut sugar to the boil and then simmer for 2 minutes, until thick and shiny. Mix in the cream and add the sea salt.

5 Blanch the chard in a pan of boiling water for 1 minute. Drain and dry. Arrange the chard in the pastry case in a circular pattern starting from the outside and working inwards, and then drizzle over the caramel sauce.

6 Bake for 15 minutes, then cool a little before removing to a wire rack. Serve warm or cool, decorated with flowers.

Parsnip Upside Down Tarte

Tarte tatin is traditionally baked with the topping underneath so that it caramelises, and then flipped over to serve - a luscious rich pudding tart that's perfect for parsnips.

Apples or pears are the usual go-to fruits for this dessert cake, with pineapples also frequently used, but it's the special caramelising properties of parsnips that win them the star spot in this recipe.

The base is paleo, spongy, and gently flavoured, letting the parsnips and spices take centre stage on a fluffy bed of almonds, potato and buckwheat.

Parsnips are commonplace in the UK, but in many other countries they're unusual and regarded as exotic. When I arrived in California, nobody I met had heard of parsnips. Scouring the farmer's markets, I finally found some, and they were met with gasps and exclamations of "white carrots!". This isn't totally off the mark, as they are indeed in the same family as carrots, but as you know, they're definitely something else. One of their greatest attributes is their ability to caramelise into intensely sticky and toffee-flavoured hues, which is what we're interested in here. Serve this with ice cream or custard for a nostalgic dessert, albeit one with a modern twist.

MAKES ONE 23CM/9IN TARTE, SERVES 6-8

80g/3¼ oz/generous ½ cup potato flour

50g/2oz/½ cup buckwheat flour

50g/2oz/½ cup ground blanched almonds

37.5ml/2½ tbsp arrowroot

15ml/1 tbsp baking powder

5ml/1 tsp ground cinnamon

2.5ml/½ tsp ground ginger

1.5ml/¼ tsp pink or sea salt

175ml/6fl oz/¾ cup almond milk

15ml/1 tbsp apple cider vinegar

225g/8oz/1 cup/2 sticks unsalted butter, at room temperature

150g/5oz/¾ cup coconut sugar

2 eggs

½ nutmeg, grated, or 2.5ml/½ tsp ground

5ml/1 tsp ground turmeric

3-4 parsnips, peeled and cut into thick strips

Coconut cream or custard, to serve (optional)

1 Preheat the oven to 160°C/325°F/Gas 3.

2 In a medium bowl, sift together the potato and buckwheat flours, ground almonds, arrowroot, baking powder, cinnamon, ginger and salt.

3 In a jug or cup, mix together the almond milk and the vinegar.

4 In another bowl, cream together half of the butter and half of the sugar using a spoon. Next, using an electric whisk set to medium, add the eggs one by one to the butter mixture, with roughly a spoonful of the dry mixture added along with each egg.

5 Keep whisking, and add the dry flour mix and the soured almond milk mix, little by little, alternating until both are incorporated into the batter. Set aside.

6 In a 23cm/9in cast iron skillet or deep ovenproof frying pan, heat the remaining butter over a low heat until it liquefies and the foam subsides, leaving brown butter. Add the rest of the coconut sugar, the nutmeg and turmeric.

7 Add the parsnips, and turn them in the butter mixture to coat them well, then arrange them nicely in an even layer – this is how they will appear on your finished cake.

8 Cover and cook on low for about 3–5 minutes, until the parsnips are slightly softened and are starting to absorb the flavoured butter mixture.

9 Pour the cake mixture over the top of the layer of parsnips, and transfer the skillet or pan to the oven.

10 Bake for 45 minutes, until the cake is golden brown and a skewer inserted into the middle comes out clean. Allow to cool for about 10 minutes, then loosen the sides by running a knife around the edge of the skillet. Place a serving plate over the top of the pan, then turn it upside down to release the cake.

11 Serve warm or cool with coconut cream (or custard).

Courgette Rosette Tart

A delicate gluten-free pastry shell filled with a coconut maple crème anglaise, and topped with pretty courgette rosettes and an optional wine glaze.

The crust of this tart is buttery and sweet, beautifully complementing a silky custard inside. The custard includes tapioca; it's more robust than usual tart fillings, but still silky smooth. There is an optional wine glaze to give a sheen – if you use green courgettes, a red wine would add a rosy tint.

The courgette rosettes curled over the top aren't baked – they're totally raw. It's a lovely late summer or early autumn tart.

MAKES ONE 25CM/10IN TART, SERVES 10–12

250ml/8fl oz/1 cup almond milk

50ml/2fl oz/¼ cup maple syrup

45ml/3 tbsp tapioca flour

2 eggs, one of them separated

2.5ml/½ tsp vanilla extract

15ml/1 tbsp coconut oil, plus extra for greasing

125ml/4fl oz/½ cup canned coconut cream, pre-blended and chilled

3 medium courgettes (zucchini), plus a few shavings to decorate

For the wine glaze (optional)

50g/2oz/¼ cup Dutch apelstroop (apple juice spread), or sugar-free marmalade or apricot jam

30ml/2 tbsp wine

Drop of rose essential oil

For the pastry

210g/7½oz/scant 2 cups gluten-free plain (all-purpose) flour mix, plus extra for dusting

115g/4oz/½ cup/1 stick unsalted butter, cold

25g/1oz/¼ cup ground almonds

40g/1½oz/scant ¼ cup coconut sugar

1.5ml/¼ tsp pink or sea salt

1 egg

1 To make the pastry, sift the flour into a bowl, and add the butter. Rub the butter into the flour using your fingertips to create crumbs, working quickly. Add the almonds, coconut sugar and salt, and stir to combine. Add the egg, and beat it into the flour mixture using a fork. Work it all together well with your hands to form a dough.

2 Shape the dough into a disc about 10cm/4in. Cover with clear film or plastic wrap and chill the pastry in the refrigerator for about 20 minutes.

3 Lightly dust your counter with flour and grease a 25cm/10in loose-bottomed fluted tart tin (pan).

4 Roll out the pastry disc until it's 3mm/⅛in thick, then using the rolling pin, transfer it to the tart tin. Cut off any excess pastry, and patch any tears if necessary.

5 Line the pastry case with baking parchment, then fill it with baking beans or pastry weights and refrigerate for at least 20 minutes. Preheat the oven to 190°C/375°F/Gas 5.

6 Bake the pastry case for 18–20 minutes, then remove the beans and paper. Return to the oven, and bake for 5 more minutes, until the pastry looks dry.

7 Brush the inside of the pastry crust with a thin layer of the egg white (listed in the filling ingredients). Return to the oven, and bake for 2–3 minutes more, until the egg is dry and the crust is golden brown. Set aside to cool on a rack.

8 To make the maple crème Anglaise, heat the almond milk in a pan over a low heat.

9 In a heatproof bowl, whisk the maple syrup and tapioca flour with the whole egg and the remaining egg yolk, using a fork or a hand whisk.

10 Add about half the hot almond milk, and keep whisking to combine, then pour all of the liquid back into the pan. Keep whisking, and turn the heat up to bring to the boil.

(continued overleaf)

11 Keep whisking and boiling for about a minute to make sure the crème is thick, then remove it from the heat and whisk in the vanilla and coconut oil.

12 Transfer the crème back to the bowl, cover, and set aside to cool completely, about 2 hours or more; it will keep in the fridge until needed for up to 3 days.

13 When ready for the next step, whisk the chilled coconut cream using an electric whisk on high until the cream is whipped.

14 Stir the crème Anglaise to make it fluid and creamy again, then add it little by little to the coconut cream, whisking to combine.

15 Transfer into the pastry shell, smooth down, and chill again for about an hour.

16 Next, make the courgette rosettes by making ribbon strips of raw courgette using a vegetable peeler, that are about equal thickness, and place them in a bowl of water to keep them fresh.

17 Curl the courgettes into themselves, adding another layer of ribbon as needed to form the rosette size you like, then place each rosette into the bed of crème. Continue until the pastry case is full of rolled courgette rosettes.

18 Chill, and serve cold within a day of preparing the courgette rosettes.

VARIATION: WINE GLAZE

To add a wine glaze, combine the apelstroop, wine and essential oil, if using, in a small pan over a low heat, and whisk with a fork. Before the final chilling, paint the courgette rosettes with the wine jelly. If you use red wine it will tint the courgettes pink as well as adding sweetness and sheen – this would look better on green courgettes than yellow.

Broccoli Custard Flan Slices

Full of eggs, butter and wheat flour, this is a very custardy and old-fashioned bake, with delicate spears of purple or green broccoli adding a contrasting bite.

These more-ish layered slices have a flan pastry base, a creamy filling of warm vanilla notes mingled with maple sugar, and a delicious brown caramelised topping. This dessert needs no ice cream or pouring cream as an accompaniment, but if you want to add a little something, why not grate some white chocolate on top and sprinkle with some dried coconut strands? And play some old trad jazz as you cut into it with a pastry fork. Serve with linen napkins! These slices are also perfect for a posh picnic.

MAKES 6–8 SLICES

115g/4 oz green or purple sprouting broccoli

30ml/2 tbsp unsalted butter, plus extra for greasing

150g/5oz/¾ cup maple sugar

750ml/1¼ pints/3 cups full-fat (whole) milk

5ml/1 tsp vanilla extract or 1 vanilla pod (bean), split

4 eggs

50g/2oz/½ cup cornflour (cornstarch)

For the pastry

115g/4oz/½ cup/1 stick unsalted butter, frozen

150g/5 oz/1¼ cups plain (all-purpose) flour, plus extra for dusting

30ml/2 tbsp maple sugar

1.5ml/¼ tsp pink or sea salt

75ml/5 tbsp iced water

1 Grease a 15 x 20cm/6 x 8in baking tin (pan) and line it with baking parchment.

2 To make the pastry, grate the frozen butter into a bowl and sift in the flour, and stir in the maple sugar and salt. Using your fingertips, rub the butter into the flour mixture to form crumbs.

3 Little by little, add the water until a dough forms. You may not have to use all of the water. Keep kneading the dough until it is smooth, but not sticky. Form the dough into a ball, and wrap it with clear film or plastic wrap, then place in the refrigerator for an hour, or overnight.

4 When ready, dust the counter with flour, unwrap the pastry, and roll it out into a disc that's about 5mm/¼in thick. Using your rolling pin to help, transfer the pastry into the tin, and press it into the base.

5 Slice the broccoli thinly lengthways, then put the butter into a frying pan and melt it on a medium heat with a teaspoon of the maple sugar. When the butter starts to froth, add the broccoli strips and coat with the butter, using a spatula to turn them.

6 Turn down the heat to low, and put the lid on. Sauté for about 6–8 minutes, until the broccoli is cooked to the desired softness. Set aside to cool. Preheat the oven to 180°C/350°F/Gas 4.

7 Pour the milk into a small heavy pan, add the vanilla, and heat gently over a low heat until it's warm, but not boiling. If using a vanilla pod, take the pan off the heat, add the pod and allow to infuse for about 20 minutes, then discard the pod. If using extract simply add to the milk at this point.

8 In a bowl, whisk the eggs, the rest of the maple sugar and the cornflour together with a hand whisk.

9 Put the milk back on a medium heat, and when it starts to boil, add the egg mixture in a slow stream, whisking it constantly as it's poured. As soon as large bubbles begin to appear around the sides of the pan, take the custard off the heat and pour it over the pastry base.

10 Bake for about 1 hour, until the top is brown and the filling only slightly wiggles in the centre of the flan when you gently shake the pan from side to side.

11 While still warm, arrange the caramelised broccoli over the top. Allow to fully cool in the tin before taking it out, cutting into slices and serving.

Red Romanesco Tart

With the tips of pink-hued Romanesco cauliflower on top of pink cream clouds, this is a visually intense dessert, full of romantic, psychedelic splendour.

Romanesco fronds are poached in a raspberry coulis, colouring them in addition to imparting juicy tartness. The coulis is infused with cardamom, cinnamon and star anise, and the acidity of the raspberries is a vehicle for these, as well as the lemon juice. The Moroccan-inspired combination of spices seems fitting for such a beautiful swirl of vegetables.

The pastry case is made with ground almonds, so it's paleo. It has a lovely marzipan flavour, but has the crispness of a more traditional pastry. It's filled with pink fluffy coconut cream, whipped to perfection with more of the raspberry coulis.

You could replace the raspberries with pomegranate juice instead, for a deeper colour and stronger flavour.

MAKES ONE 23CM/9IN TART, SERVES 10–12

- 2–3 Romanesco cauliflowers (roughly 250g/9oz)
- 140g/5oz/1 cup fresh raspberries
- 120ml/4fl oz/½ cup honey
- Juice and zest of 1 lemon
- 500ml/17fl oz/generous 2 cups water
- 8 cardamom pods
- 2 cinnamon sticks
- 2 star anise
- 400ml/14fl oz/1 can of coconut cream, chilled

For the pastry
- 225g/8oz/2 cups ground almonds
- Pinch of pink or sea salt
- 30ml/2 tbsp coconut oil
- 1 egg

1 Preheat the oven to 180°C/350°F/Gas 4. To make the pastry, place the ground almonds and salt in a food processor, and pulse for ten seconds to combine. Add the coconut oil and egg, and pulse, stopping every now and then to clean down the sides of the bowl. Continue until the dough has combined, which will take about a minute.

2 Using a wooden spoon, press the dough into a 23cm/9in ovenproof pie dish. Bake for 10 minutes, until golden and dry. Take out of the oven and leave to cool.

3 Meanwhile, cut away any leaves and the core from the Romanesco and then separate it into individual fronds, keeping the shapes as much as possible.

4 In a blender, process the raspberries, honey, lemon juice and water. Pour the raspberry liquid into a large pan and add the cardamom, cinnamon, star anise and zest.

5 Gently lower the Romanesco into the liquid, and bring to a simmer over a medium heat. Cover the top of the pan with a piece of baking parchment, put the lid on, and turn the heat down to low. Leave to slowly simmer for about 5–7 minutes, depending on how soft you'd like the Romanesco to be. Make sure it's not so soft that it disintegrates.

6 Turn off the heat, and either gently lift the Romanesco out with a slotted spoon, or let it continue to sit in the warm raspberry coulis, where it will cook a little more.

7 Open the can of cold coconut cream, and drain off the liquid to make it thicker. Scoop out the semi-solid white coconut cream and place in a bowl. Add two tablespoons of the raspberry coulis, and beat with an electric whisk for about 4–5 minutes until it is blended and whipped.

8 Spoon the pink coconut cream into the pastry case, then gently arrange the fronds of Romanesco on top.

9 Chill in the refrigerator to set for at least half an hour, then serve cold with the remaining raspberry coulis drizzled over.

COOK'S TIP
It's possible to make the paleo pastry by hand, but it works best using a food processor as the ground almonds are pulverised further as well as combining thoroughly with the egg and coconut oil.

Fiddlehead Fern Galette Tart

Extremely seasonal, fiddlehead ferns are available for no more than a month every year, and are something to leap on if you are lucky enough to find them locally to you.

Foraged not farmed, you might see these ferns in farmers' markets or special greengrocers (or on a walk!). They only grow in climates with marked seasons, as they need a cold winter as much as a mild spring. Slowly they emerge from their wintery slumber under the forest floor, bright spring-green feathered with brown fuzzy down, like a deer's antlers. Left to unfurl, they become prehistoric leafy ferns, but if they're cut while still in a spiral, they're a tender local delicacy that can't be forgotten. Wherever your ancestors originated, there's a primal element to preparing and eating fiddleheads. There is the scent as they steam, their delicate green taste, and then there are the curls…

The gluten-free vegan pastry has cornmeal to add to the rusticity, and fennel seeds for bursts of flavour. You can make this in a pie dish or form directly onto a baking sheet for a more rustic galette.

MAKES ONE 23CM/9IN TART, SERVES 6-8

500g/1¼lb fiddlehead ferns, washed thoroughly to remove any grit

5ml/1 tsp fennel pollen

5ml/1 tsp dried tarragon or 10ml/2 tsp fresh tarragon, chopped, plus fresh sprigs to decorate

30ml/2 tbsp cornflour (cornstarch)

Juice and zest of ½ lemon

30ml/2 tbsp coconut oil, melted, plus extra for greasing

75ml/2½fl oz/⅓ cup maple syrup (or honey if acceptable)

For the pastry

120g/4oz/1 cup gluten-free plain (all-purpose) flour mix

50g/2oz/½ cup cornmeal

30ml/2 tbsp coconut sugar

Pinch of pink or sea salt, plus extra for decorating

10ml/2 tsp fennel seeds, crushed

115g/4oz/½ cup vegan margarine, frozen

approx 90ml/3fl oz/6 tbsp iced water

15ml/1 tbsp hemp milk, for glazing

1 To make the pastry, in a large bowl, mix together the flour, cornmeal, coconut sugar, salt and fennel seeds. Grate the frozen margarine into the bowl, and mix it in. Add the iced water little by little, to form a dough. You may not need all of the water to make a good consistency pastry, depending on the absorbency of the flour.

2 Bring the dough together into a ball with your hands, and flatten it to form a disc. Wrap the disc in clear film or plastic wrap, and chill in the refrigerator for at least 1 hour, or overnight.

3 When you're ready for the next step, preheat the oven to 180°C/350°F/Gas 4.

4 Unwrap and roll out the pastry to a rough circle. Grease a 23cm/9in ovenproof dish and line it with pastry, letting the edges overhang without cutting it off. Or, lay the pastry flat on a greased baking sheet for a traditional galette.

5 Bring a pan of water to boil and add the fiddlehead ferns. Allow to blanch for about 5 minutes, then remove the ferns and plunge them into a bowl of iced water.

6 Mix the fennel pollen, tarragon, cornflour, lemon juice and zest, coconut oil and maple syrup in a jug or cup.

7 Drain the ferns, put them in a bowl and drizzle with the fennel-syrup mixture. Using a wooden spoon, turn the ferns gently to coat them as evenly as possible.

8 Place the fiddlehead ferns evenly in the pastry case, leaving about 2.5cm/1in gap around the edges. Fold the edges of the pastry over to form a border if you like and brush with hemp milk.

9 Bake for 40 minutes, until the pastry is golden brown. Allow to cool in the pie dish. Sprinkle with sprigs of fresh tarragon and some extra salt.

10 If you like, serve this spring dessert with a light ale to complete the medieval feel of the whole experience, or a nice hot mug of fennel tea.

Brussels Hazelnut Frangipane Tart

Autumn's most beloved flavours include Brussels sprouts, hazelnuts, buckwheat and a fine bourbon whisky. Who wouldn't agree with that?

In this tart, I've created a buckwheat flour pastry stage for the Brussels to star on. And first, I've dressed the set with an outrageous hazelnut whisky frangipane with sticky medjool dates, and smothered everything in butter.

This is not a slimming dessert! It has nothing to do with abstemiousness. That said, it can't be considered unhealthy. On the contrary, it's a sleek delivery system for the most potent cruciferous vegetable, the tiny leaves being rich with antioxidants, folates and vitamin C, not to mention fibre. You'd never guess this from the crisp crumb of the buttery buckwheat pastry, it all seems so crumbly and naughty.

And hazelnuts! A distinctly European flavour, here paired with an American whisky. We are so lucky to be cooking at this time in history, with access to a wild diversity of ingredients from every time and place, a luxury our great-grandparents and even grandparents couldn't imagine.

MAKES ONE 23CM/9IN TART, SERVES 8–10

225g/8oz Brussels sprouts, trimmed and outer leaves removed, and quartered

280g/10oz/1 cup hazelnuts

4 pitted (stoned) medjool dates

25ml/1½ tbsp bourbon whisky

50g/2oz/¼ cup/½ stick butter, at room temperature, plus extra for greasing

For the pastry

40g/1½oz/generous ¼ cup buckwheat flour

40g/1½oz/generous ¼ cup gluten-free plain (all-purpose) flour mix, plus extra for dusting

Pinch of pink or sea salt

115g/4oz/½ cup/1 stick butter, frozen

30ml/2 tbsp iced water

30ml/2 tbsp hazelnut milk, for glazing

1 First make the pastry by sifting the flours into a bowl with the salt. Grate the butter into the bowl, and combine into the flour using your fingertips. Add the water little by little, and make the dough into a ball with your hands. Flatten the ball into a disc that's about 13cm/5in wide. Wrap with clear film or plastic wrap, and chill for at least an hour, or overnight.

2 When you're ready to make the tart, first leave the pastry on the counter to warm a little, for about 15 minutes. Preheat the oven to 200°C/400°F/Gas 6 and grease a 23cm/9in fluted, loose-bottomed pie tin (pan). On a clean surface dusted with flour, roll out the pastry to a little bigger than the tin. Place the pastry into the tin and trim around the edge of the tart to neaten, cutting a little higher than the tin.

3 Cover with baking parchment and fill with baking beans and bake blind for 10 minutes. Remove the parchment and beans and cook for a further 5 minutes. Remove the tart and turn the oven down to 180°C/350°F/Gas 4.

4 Bring a pan of water to boil, blanch the quartered Brussels for 5–6 minutes, then plunge into a bowl of ice water before draining.

5 Roast the hazelnuts for 8–10 minutes, until the skins are just splitting. Transfer the nuts to a high-speed blender, and process on the highest setting to form a paste, scraping the sides of the bowl with a spatula. Add the dates, bourbon and butter, and whizz again to combine into a smooth paste.

6 Transfer the Brussels to a bowl along with the hazelnut mixture. Combine well using a spatula, then spread over the pastry shell. Brush the pastry border with hazelnut milk. Bake for 30–35 minutes, until the crust is golden.

7 Leave to cool in the tin for 5–10 minutes, then remove carefully and cool on a rack for a further 20 minutes.

8 Serve warm, or allow to cool completely and serve cold – maybe with hazelnut ice cream and a cup of Irish coffee.

Maple Lemon Veggie Slab Pie

This is an all-out vegetable pie – but sweet! A slab pie is made in a shallow oblong pan, and this particular one with late summer vegetables tastes of maple syrup and lemon.

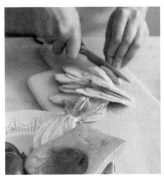   

A whole lemon is used inside the creamy filling, so the flavour isn't just the sharpness of lemon juice. It's much rounder and more complex than that, including the deep tones of the zest.

The red pepper becomes sweet as it bakes, as do the fennel, celeriac and butternut squash. This book is about re-thinking the obvious, re-examining the preconceived ideas we all have about the simple things around us, like the idea that vegetables are savoury and fruit is sweet. This pie proves the point; nothing is quite as it seems at first glance.

SERVES 6–8

1 lemon, unwaxed

100ml/3½fl oz/scant ½ cup maple syrup

1 red (bell) pepper, cored and chopped

100g/3¾oz celeriac (celery root), peeled and sliced

1 small bulb fennel, sliced

350g/12oz butternut squash, peeled and grated

For the pastry

250g/9oz/2 cups plain (all-purpose) flour, plus extra for dusting

150g/5oz/¾ cup/1½ sticks chilled unsalted butter, cubed, plus extra for greasing

15ml/1 tbsp maple syrup

1 egg, separated

30ml/2 tbsp iced water

1 First make the pastry. In a large bowl, combine the flour and butter. Rub the butter into the flour with your fingertips until fully integrated. Then add the 15ml/1 tbsp of maple syrup, the egg yolk and about 30ml/2 tbsp very cold water. Stir then bring together into a dough with your hands. Knead in the bowl for 5 minutes until smooth. Wrap the dough in clear film or plastic wrap and chill for 1 hour.

2 In the meantime, cover the lemon with boiling water in a small pan and bring to the boil. Simmer on high for 15 minutes, or until the lemon is soft. Drain the water and use as stock for another recipe or freeze. Remove the pips from the lemon and then liquidise in a blender. Blend in the 100ml/3½fl oz maple syrup.

3 Preheat the oven to 200°C/400°F/Gas 6 and grease a 25 x 20cm/10 x 8in baking tin (pan). Cut two thirds away from the pastry and roll out on a clean surface lightly dusted with flour to fit the tin. Chill for 30 minutes.

4 Fill the pastry case with the vegetables, then pour over the lemon mixture. Roll out the remaining pastry to roughly 21 x 15cm/6 x 8½in, then cut long strips and lay them in a criss-cross pattern on top of the vegetables, securing by pressing down on the edges.

5 Beat the egg white and brush the pastry with it to glaze. Bake for 25 minutes, or until the vegetables are cooked and the pastry is golden. Serve warm or cool.

Cookies

Yes, we have cookies... which encompasses a wider selection of baked goods than one might first imagine. We have the crisp, flat kind that go well with a cup of tea, but there's everything else too from flat cakes to flapjacks. And of course, there is something a bit different and vegetabley about all of them, whether it's the green-ness of the Kale Matcha Cookies, and Spinach Macarons, or the super-soft flour-free Cakey Cauli Cookies. Some use more traditional ingredients (pumpkin, carrot), and some quite surprising ones. You will need to don a pair of gloves to collect wild stinging nettles for the Nettle Biscotti, but will be rewarded by the wildest, freshest and superb-tasting biscuits. Many recipes are gluten-free, nut-free and refined sugar-free, and there are even egg-free macaroons (and macarons!), made with the exciting 'secret' ingredient, aquafaba, which I've included in a few of the recipes in this book. And to complete the collection, the Parsnip, Swede and Hazelnut Flapjacks are sumptuous. I'm a massive flapjack fan, and these ones don't fail to deliver on oaty goodness mixed with soft, sweet, starchy vegetables. They're excellent, and a handy treat to keep on hand for those moments when you need a quick snack. All in all I'm confident there's a cookie of every kind and for every occasion to be found within this chapter.

Corn, Sage and Apricot Cookies

These are two-corn cookies made from a base of corn, in the form of polenta, and fresh juicy sweet corn kernels, alongside chopped dried apricots.

Butter cookies, sweetened with coconut sugar; these have a crisp crumb that's made more rustic with the polenta. They are flavoured with sage to perfectly bridge the seasons from summer into autumn.

They're an excellent tea cookie, and make great dunkers. They're also fantastic as a sweet cheese cracker, making a delicious base for mild cheeses like cheddar or gouda, and for accompaniments like quince jelly.

Store them in an airtight container, and eat within a week to ensure crispness.

MAKES 25 COOKIES

1 ear or cob of fresh corn	5ml/1 tsp baking powder
3 dried apricots	1.5ml/¼ tsp pink or sea salt
5ml/1 tsp dried sage, crushed	80g/3¾oz/⅓ cup/¾ stick unsalted butter, softened
100g/3¾oz/1 cup plain (all-purpose) flour	70g/2½ oz/⅓ cup coconut sugar
50g/2oz/½ cup polenta	2 eggs

1 Remove the husks and hair from the corn, then lay down flat on a chopping board, and cut the kernels off using a sharp knife, rotating the cob to remove all of them. Discard the inside and outside material, and put the kernels into a medium bowl.

2 Finely chop the apricots, and add them to the bowl along with the sage, then combine with a fork.

3 In a medium bowl, sift together the flour, polenta, baking powder and salt, adding back into the bowl any husk that may remain in the sieve or strainer. Set aside.

4 In a separate bowl, cream the butter and coconut sugar together with a wooden spoon. Add the eggs one at a time, adding a tablespoon of the flour mixture along with each egg.

5 Mix the rest of the flour mixture and the corn mixture into the batter, and combine first with the spoon, and then with your hands.

6 Put the dough back into a clean bowl, cover closely with baking parchment, clear film or plastic wrap, and allow to rest in the refrigerator for an hour, or for up to a week if you want to prepare ahead.

7 When you're ready to bake the cookies, set the oven to 160°C/325°F/Gas 3. Line a baking sheet with baking parchment.

8 Form little dough balls that are about the size of a fresh apricot, then flatten each of them gently on to the baking sheet. You'll have about 25 cookies.

9 Bake in the centre of the oven for about 6 minutes, then turn the sheet and bake for about 6 more minutes, until light golden brown.

VARIATION
Leave out the sage, and replace with 5ml/1 tsp ground cinnamon instead for a more familiar flavour.

Kale Matcha Cookies

Kale, kale, kale. You may have noticed, it's been having a bit of a moment.
As has matcha tea.

So... it seemed imperative to give you this on-trend recipe that's doubly green due to copious amounts of fresh kale and matcha tea.

These cookies are made with spelt flour so they're low in gluten, and contain a generous amount of butter, so they melt in the mouth and taste delicious. Pretty much anything is guaranteed to taste good when it's a cookie made with butter and coconut sugar, right?

Cut these cookies into pretty shapes using your favourite cookie cutters, and you'll be ready to eat them within an hour of first thinking it would be a nice idea to have a kale matcha cookie to go with your cup of matcha tea.

MAKES ABOUT 20 COOKIES

- 15g/½oz kale leaves, such as dinosaur or Lacinato, stalks removed
- 115g/4oz/½ cup/1 stick unsalted butter, at room temperature
- 2.5ml/½ tsp vanilla extract
- 140g/4¾ oz/scant ¾ cup coconut sugar
- 185g/6oz/1½ cups spelt flour, plus extra for dusting
- 25g/1oz/¼ cup matcha tea powder, plus extra for dusting
- 25g/1oz/¼ cup ground flax seeds
- 2.5ml/½ tsp pink or sea salt, plus extra crushed for sprinkling

1 In a food processor or blender, process the kale with just enough hot water to allow it to purée, about a tablespoon or two depending on the speed of the blender and the juiciness of the leaves.

2 In a mixing bowl, cream together the butter, vanilla and coconut sugar using a spoon. Add the kale purée and combine.

3 Sift in the spelt flour, matcha tea, flax seeds and salt, re-adding any larger particles that are caught in the sieve or strainer. Mix the dry ingredients into the wet first with the spoon, and then using your hands to create a dough.

4 Roll the dough into a ball and cover with a clean cloth. Chill in the refrigerator for at least 30 minutes.

5 When you're ready to bake the cookies, preheat the oven to 180°C/350°F/Gas 4. Line a large baking sheet with baking parchment.

6 Dust a surface and rolling pin with spelt flour, and roll out the dough until it's 1cm/½in thick.

7 Cut into pretty shapes using a cookie cutter, and transfer the cookies to the baking sheet. Bake for 15–20 minutes, until the edges are just starting to turn brown.

8 Allow to cool for a few minutes on the sheet, then transfer to a cooling rack using a spatula. Sprinkle over a little crushed salt if you like.

VARIATIONS

Instead of using mature kale leaves and removing the stalks, use baby kale or baby spinach for a milder flavour. You'll need to use a little more water to make a purée. Instead of water to purée the leaves, you could use a little hot matcha tea for a stronger flavour.

Pumpkin Cookies

This is an all-American cookie, from the pumpkin to the sunflower butter. I suggest them for children, but of course they are popular with all ages.

Gluten-free, nut-free and sugar-free, so perfect for a children's birthday party as there's no need to warn anyone about anything they might be allergic to. What's more, they're vegan! Quick and simple to make, these moist cookies are delicious, with a tender texture, and classic taste from the traditional pumpkin spice mixture. I'm usually a stickler for cooking everything from scratch, but to be honest, pumpkin purée out of the can is your best bet for these cookies, as they're such a staple kind of treat. They can be made in 20 minutes from opening a can to serving them warm. Now that's fun, and the simplest way to get some vegetable on to a plate with the guarantee that it will be eaten up! And if there are any left over, they can be stored in an airtight tin for up to a week.

1 Preheat the oven to 180°C/350°F/Gas 4. Grease and line a large baking sheet with baking parchment.

2 In a bowl, mix all of the ingredients together using a wooden spoon. Pull off pieces of dough, and roll into balls roughly 2.5cm/1in.

3 Press the balls to flatten them one by one on to the baking sheet.

4 Bake until golden brown, about 12–15 minutes. The longer they bake, the crisper they'll become, so if you prefer a chewy biscuit, take them out sooner.

5 Allow to cool completely on a cooling rack, and sprinkle with coconut if using.

    NF DF VG SF GF

MAKES ABOUT 12 COOKIES

180g/6¼ oz/2 cups rolled oats

250g/9oz/1 cup pumpkin purée

115g/4oz/½ cup sunflower butter

50g/2oz/¼ cup coconut sugar

1.5ml/¼ tsp baking powder

1.5ml/¼ tsp ground nutmeg

1.5ml/¼ tsp ground coriander

1.5ml/¼ tsp ground cardamom

1.5ml/¼ tsp ground cinnamon

Desiccated raw (dry unsweetened macaroon-cut shredded) coconut, for sprinkling (optional)

Spinach Macarons

These have the appearance and texture of classic French macarons but that's where convention ends, being made with aquafaba and full of green spinachy goodness.

These macarons are filled with sun-dried tomato, cream cheese, and fresh basil. Basil is becoming more widely used in sweet recipes, and rightly so. Its fragrant quality is a natural partner for desserts, and it's perfect with cream cheese and tomato.

The vegetable component is spinach, in the form of powder – homemade spinach powder that's dried at a low heat in the oven. It's a fantastic ingredient for a wide variety of uses, so feel free to make too much while you're doing this, and keep it in an airtight jar ready to use – whether to colour future frostings or simply to sprinkle over your dinners. It's extremely versatile. I thoroughly recommend including the Versawhip, as listed. It's a soy protein extract powder that is magic for keeping aquafaba foams robust and creamy. It's hard to find in stores, but it's available online in most countries, and really is a way to ensure your meringue mixture is a good consistency. This recipe is one of the most challenging ones in this book, so set aside some time – you'll be pleased with the end result.

 GF

MAKES 20 SANDWICHED MACARONS

Bunch of mature spinach, stalks and midribs removed

150g/5oz/1¼ cups blanched almond flour

150g/5oz/¾ cup granulated (white) sugar

175ml/6 fl oz/⅔ cup aquafaba i.e. the liquid from a can of chickpeas

Juice of ⅛ lemon, i.e. a small wedge

1.5ml/¼ tsp Versawhip, or other soy protein (optional)

For the filling

60ml/4 tbsp sun-dried tomato paste, unsalted

30ml/2 tbsp cream cheese, at room temperature

15ml/1 tbsp clear honey

20 fresh basil leaves

1 First, wash the spinach well and dry it thoroughly, using a salad spinner or a cloth set on a rack so the leaves can properly dry.

2 Set the oven to the lowest setting, and find a non-combustible object such as a silicone spatula or a ball of foil that can be used to keep the door ajar.

3 Place the spinach leaves on pieces of baking parchment in a single layer, being careful the leaves don't overlap, then put them in the oven for about 1–1½ hours until they are dehydrated. Allow to cool on the paper, then pulverise in a high-speed blender.

4 Measure out 10g/¼oz of the spinach powder, and store the rest in an airtight container for future use. (It suits everything from smoothies to salads, and of course, in vegetable cakes!)

5 Line a large baking sheet with baking parchment.

6 Put the almond flour, half of the sugar, and the 10g/¼oz of spinach powder in a high-speed blender, and process for about 10 seconds to create a superfine blended powder. Be careful not to over-blend, as the almond flour will liquefy and become a paste after too long.

7 Tip the powdered almond flour, sugar and spinach into a sieve or strainer that's suspended over a bowl, and sift to remove any large particles.

(continued overleaf)

8 Pour the aquafaba into a separate bowl and squeeze in the lemon juice. Whisk the aquafaba with the remaining sugar and Versawhip, if using, with an electric whisk set to high. Keep beating until it forms stiff peaks, about 5 minutes.

9 Slowly and carefully, little by little, fold the almond mixture into the whipped mixture using a spatula. Be very careful not to disturb the airy whipped foam you've made; if you beat the air out of the batter at this stage, the macarons won't work, so be careful and take your time folding. The mixture should form ribbons when dropped from the spatula. It's important the consistency is perfect at this stage – too wet, and the macaron 'feet' won't develop; too dry, and the tops will crack.

10 Using a small round piping nozzle, transfer the mixture into an piping bag, clip the top, and pipe little 2.5cm/1in macarons on to the baking sheet, keeping the bag vertical, and making sure the macarons are evenly spaced out on the sheet.

11 Put the sheet of macarons into the oven, but don't turn the oven on yet. Leave them in the oven to set overnight before proceeding to the next stage.

12 When ready to bake the next day, remove the sheet carefully and preheat the oven to 100°C/200°F/Gas ¼, making sure not to set the fan-function if there is one.

13 When the oven is heated, place the macarons inside on the middle shelf, and bake for 20 minutes.

14 Don't take the macarons out, but turn the oven off and leave them to continue cooking in the residual heat for another 15 minutes.

15 Open the oven door but leave the macarons inside for another 15 minutes.

16 Finally remove the sheet from the oven and leave them to cool.

17 While they're cooling make the tomato paste filling by blending the sun-dried tomatoes, cream cheese and honey together in a jug or cup with a spoon.

18 Pipe or spread the bottom of two macarons with tomato paste. Sandwich a basil leaf in between them. Repeat for all of the macarons, gently placing each on a plate when ready.

19 Chill the sandwiched macarons in the refrigerator for at least 24 hours before serving.

COOK'S TIPS

Don't be tempted to use silicone mats instead of baking parchment, as the macarons will shrink a little as they bake, resulting in an odd shape and no 'feet'. Likewise, foil will mess them up.

If you can, don't serve these on the day they're baked. They are best filled and kept for 24 hours before serving.

Finally, the innovative aquafaba is a wonderful substitute for egg white, but don't be tempted to use anything other than refined cane sugar. Unfortunately replacements like coconut sugar simply dissolve and don't do the job of creating architecture that standard cane sugar does as it bakes. It's here for structure as much as for sweetness.

Cakey Cauli Cookies

These are exactly as they sound. Cookie-cakes made with cauliflower. They're spicy, soft, and extremely more-ish – as well as being deliciously easy to make.

The cauliflower flavour is a wonderful, subtle frame for the cinnamon and ginger spice mix, but goes particularly well with nutmeg, which never fails to enhance the sulfurous notes in this ubiquitous vegetable. This cookbook is all about how to use everyday vegetables in ways we never previously considered, despite us being so familiar with them.

Your family and friends, like mine, will go from 'yuck to yum' within one bite of eating these. And with that, they will open up to all the other creative ideas. I mean, if you can replace flour with the grated shreds of a head of cauliflower to make cookies, what else can you do?

Onto the texture. If a cookie by definition needs to be hard and crispy, then these must be cakes? But these are small and flat – perhaps we need a new compound word, like cakey-cookies.

Whatever you plump to call them, it's important you allow them to cool before attempting to pick them up, as they're not hard and crisp like regular cookies. For this reason, also take caution if you plan to dunk them as they are more like dunking a madeleine or a financier, if no less enjoyable for being so soft and cakey.

MAKES 12 COOKIES

1 medium cauliflower

125g/4¼oz/1¾ cup desiccated raw (dry unsweetened macaroon-cut shredded) coconut

50g/2oz/½ cup cornflour (cornstarch)

50g/2oz/¼ cup coconut sugar

5ml/1 tsp ground cinnamon

2.5ml/½ tsp ground ginger

1.5ml/¼ tsp ground nutmeg

2.5ml/½ tsp bicarbonate of soda (baking soda)

1 egg, beaten

80ml/3fl oz/generous ⅓ cup coconut nectar syrup

1 Set the oven to 220°C/425°F/Gas 7. Line two baking sheets with baking parchment.

2 Remove the florets from the cauliflower using a sharp knife on a cutting board. Cut the florets at the place where the individual stems start to branch into multiple tiny stems.

3 Reserve some pieces for topping but process the rest of the cauliflower tips in a food processor or blender on the lowest setting, until it is finely minced into the smallest pieces you can make, and resembles finely chopped nuts. You'll need 270g/9½oz/2 cups of processed cauliflower, so you may have a little left over (it can always be eaten raw in a salad!).

4 After you've measured it out, take a clean dish cloth, and lay it flat on the counter. Transfer the cauliflower on to the cloth, and pull up the side. Twist the closed cloth over the sink so that the cauliflower becomes tightly squeezed, and the juice can be squeezed out. You may need to do this a few times, opening and repositioning the cauliflower so that when you twist the top again, the ball of cauliflower is squeezed again on a dry area of cloth. Keep squeezing until there's no more moisture left.

5 Transfer the cauliflower to a mixing bowl, and add the coconut, cornflour, coconut sugar, spices and bicarbonate of soda. Mix well with a spatula. Add the egg and the nectar syrup, and mix well again.

6 Spoon out the batter on to the baking sheets, spacing the cookies at least 5cm/2in apart, as they will spread as they bake. Top with the reserved cauliflower tips.

7 Bake in the hot oven for about 8–10 minutes, until the cookies turn medium to dark brown around the edges.

8 Remove from the oven, and carefully slide the cookies on to a wire cooling rack. Allow to cool completely before serving, about 15 minutes.

Nettle Biscotti with Bitters

Nettles are one of our most ancient wild foods. They're native to Europe, Asia, North Africa and America, and are found everywhere from country paths to to urban backyards.

Also known as stinging nettles, of course, but don't let the sting put you off – it's immediately neutralised by cooking. Blanching stops any potential for a sting, which is why that's the first step of this recipe. However, any form of heat works. Nettles lose their sting if you sauté them in olive oil, or immerse them in boiled water to make nettle tea.

There are many different kinds of nettles; some are big and dramatic while others are tiny things. They're extremely nutritious greens, with more minerals than both broccoli and spinach, as well as being rich in vitamins, iron, and high-quality plant proteins. Just pick carefully with gloves and of course take them from an unpolluted area, avoiding roadsides. The newest leaves at the tips have the most nutrition.

These biscotti also contain another ingredient that's not often used in baking – bitters. More widely found in a cocktail, medicinal bitters are having a fashionable moment, from the well-known Angostura to many new varieties featuring single herbs and complex aromatic mixes. All of them contain the touch of bitterness that's needed for this recipe, and which enhance the natural cyanide note of the almonds. Yes – this does contain poison. (But only a little tiny bit.) Enjoy!

MAKES ABOUT 8–10 BISCOTTI

100g/3¾oz stinging nettles

Coconut oil, for greasing

2 eggs

100g/3¾oz/½ cup coconut sugar

140g/5oz ground almonds

200g/7oz/1¾ cups cornflour (cornstarch)

5ml/1 tsp bicarbonate of soda (baking soda)

2.5ml/½ tsp pink or sea salt

45ml/3 tbsp whole almonds

15ml/1 tbsp bitters

Zest of 1 lemon

1 Pick your nettles, wearing rubber gloves. Wash, then blanch the leaves and tender stems in a large pan of boiling water for 2 minutes. Plunge into cold water, drain, and dry on kitchen paper before chopping roughly.

2 Preheat the oven to 180°C/350°F/Gas 4 and grease and line a baking sheet wth baking parchment. In a food processor, whisk the eggs until light and fluffy and twice the size, then add the sugar and whisk for 2 minutes. Mix in the ground almonds, cornflour, soda and sea salt.

3 Transfer to a bowl and stir in the nettles, whole almonds, bitters and lemon zest. Mould into a loaf shape with your hands and place on the prepared sheet.

4 Bake for 20 minutes, then transfer to a chopping board and slice into strips. Lay out the strips cut-side down, on a clean baking sheet and bake again for 10 minutes. Serve.

Carrot Linzer Cookies

Linzer is the German adjective to describe something from the Austrian town of Linz. The most famous dessert from Linz is the Linzertorte, the inspiration for these cookies.

The traditional Linzertorte is a tart made from rich buttery pastry with nuts and a lattice, but there is also a mini-version called Linzersables, meaning Linzer 'eyes', and these developed over time to become Linzer cookies.

In the UK, the most famous kind of Linzer cookie is probably the commercial Jammy Dodger. Linzers are made much more frequently at home in the USA, perhaps due to the heritage of German and Austrian baking, from apple pie to spiced Christmas lebkuchen.

However, they're not generally made with vegetables, and this has now been addressed! Here are some deliciously carrot-cake-flavoured Linzer cookies for you to enjoy.

As with all Linzer cookies, they need to be eaten on the day that they are assembled in order to be enjoyed with a crisp texture. That said, many people prefer them once they have softened overnight. The decision is totally yours. Whenever you eat them, you could listen to music by Schubert or Schoenberg for the full Austrian effect.

SF

MAKES 25 COOKIES

185g/6½oz/¾ cup/1⅔ sticks softened butter, plus extra for greasing

150g/5oz/¾ cup coconut sugar, plus 30ml/2 tbsp

1 egg yolk

200g/7oz/about 2 carrots, peeled and chopped

250g/9oz/2 cups plain (all-purpose) flour, plus extra for dusting

125g/4½oz/1 cup ground almonds

5ml/1 tsp ground cinnamon, plus extra for dusting

5ml/1 tsp ground ginger

30ml/2 tbsp ground walnuts

15ml/1 tbsp pectin

30ml/2 tbsp cream cheese

1 In a large mixing bowl, cream the butter into the sugar with a spoon until fully combined. Mix in the egg yolk.

2 Liquidise the carrots until a juice-like consistency, then add two-thirds of it to the coconut sugar mixture. Stir thoroughly. Fold in the flour, almonds, cinnamon, ginger and ground walnuts, then tip on to a piece of clear film or plastic wrap and wrap up. Chill for 1 hour.

3 Grease two large flat baking sheets. Dust a clean kitchen surface with flour, then roll out half of the dough to around 30 x 40cm/12 x 16in. Using cookie cutters of your choice, cut out various shapes, making sure each cookie has an exact pair. Cut a smaller replica-shaped hole out of each cookie 'pair'.

4 Place the cookies on one baking sheet and chill while you repeat the process with the remaining dough. Then chill both sheets for 10 minutes, while you preheat the oven to 180°C/350°F/Gas 4. Bake the cookies for 12–15 minutes until golden. Allow to cool on a wire rack.

5 In a pan, bring the reserved carrot pulp and 30ml/ 2 tbsp water to the boil, then add the pectin and 2 tbsp of coconut sugar to sweeten. Boil for 5 minutes to reduce. Allow to cool slightly.

6 When the biscuits have cooled, stick the pairs together by spreading with either a thin layer of the cream cheese or the carrot mixture (or both together). Leave to set, then dust with extra ground cinnamon if you like, and serve.

Mizuna Macaroons

I've grown mizuna, and I promise you, it's incredibly easy to do. All you need is a flat tray filled with soil, and a counter that gets some sunlight.

In winter, home-grown mizuna can become your main go-to for fresh, local salad greens, wherever you live. Simply scatter seeds on soil in a pot, cover with a very thin layer of extra soil, then water and keep damp while they sprout. In a couple of weeks, you will have baby mizuna leaves ready to be snipped off with scissors. Keep the soil moist, and more mizuna will grow in its place, as if by magic.

In this sweet recipe, the mizuna is combined with the cooking water from chickpeas and some fine dried coconut to create a light yet chewy macaroon.

To be clear, these are English-style coconut macaroons, not French-style macarons, so they're easy and quick to make. Feel free to skip the final part with the chocolate topping, it's totally optional. They're delicious either way.

(NF) (DF) (SF) (VG) (GF) (PL)

MAKES 12 MACAROONS

40g/1½oz mizuna

50ml/2fl oz/¼ cup maple syrup

175ml/6fl oz/⅔ cup aquafaba i.e. the liquid from a can of chickpeas

100g/3¾oz/1½ cups desiccated raw (dry unsweetened macaroon-cut shredded) coconut

30ml/2 tbsp coconut sugar

25g/1oz chocolate, 100% cocoa solids

1 Preheat the oven to 180°C/350°F/Gas 4. Line a baking sheet with baking parchment.

2 In a blender, whizz up the mizuna and maple syrup into a fine paste. In a bowl, whisk the aquafaba with an electric whisk for 6–7 minutes until white, smooth and in peaks. Mix in the mizuna mixture, desiccated coconut and sugar with a wooden spoon.

3 Spoon mounds of the batter, each about a teaspoon and a half, on to the prepared baking sheet. Continue to do this until you use up the mixture, spacing them out about 2cm/1in apart.

4 Bake for 15–20 minutes, or until crisp and slightly coloured. Allow to cool slightly then transfer to a cooling rack to cool completely.

5 Break the chocolate into a small microwaveproof bowl. Melt in the microwave for 30 seconds, then stir. Drizzle the chocolate over the cooled macaroons, then allow to set before serving.

Parsnip, Swede and Hazelnut Flapjacks

Parsnips and swedes are quintessential Northern European winter vegetables. They are staples for the months when leafy greens are harder to come by.

These root vegetables have a texture that's great for grating, to make a mass that's substantial enough to create structure, yet soft enough so that as the flapjacks bake, they turn nice and gooey inside, while remaining pleasantly dried and oat-y on the outside.

I've suggested using date syrup for its mild sweetness, but feel free to bump up the sweetness by using maple syrup instead. It will add a lovely maple note, but may take a little longer to bake, as it's thinner than date syrup.

There's an optional dripped frosting if you feel the desire to decorate, but these are also lovely as a plain flapjack, without the added fanciness of the white coconut drizzle.

Either way, they're a wonderful treat any time of day, from being a breakfast on the go, to a snack to keep in the car.

MAKES 12 FLAPJACKS

80ml/3fl oz/⅓ cup coconut oil, plus extra for greasing

130ml/4¼fl oz/generous ½ cup date or maple syrup

100g/3¾oz/½ cup coconut sugar

225g/8oz grated parsnip

125g/4½oz grated swede (rutabaga)

325g/11½oz rolled oats

15ml/1 tbsp cornflour (cornstarch)

30ml/2 tbsp crushed hazelnuts

Zest of 1 lemon

For the drizzle frosting (optional)

Juice of ½ lemon

10g/¼oz/¼-in piece solid coconut cream block, grated

30ml/2 tbsp oat or almond milk

5ml/1 tsp maple syrup

1 Preheat the oven to 160°C/325°F/Gas 3 and grease and line a 20 x 30cm/8 x 12in rectangular baking tin (pan).

2 Place the oil in a large pan and melt until liquid. Add the date or maple syrup and coconut sugar and heat gently, stirring, for 2 minutes until it bubbles and combines.

3 In a bowl, combine the grated parsnip and swede, then mix in the oats and cornflour thoroughly. Off the heat, stir this vegetable mixture into the coconut mixture, and add the crushed hazelnuts and half of the lemon zest.

4 Transfer the mixture to the prepared tin and smooth down with the back of a wooden spoon to level. Bake for 50 minutes until golden. Allow to cool slightly, then transfer to a chopping board and cut into 12 slices.

5 To make the frosting, if using, squeeze the lemon juice over the coconut in a small bowl, and blend into a creamy paste with the back of a spoon. Add the oat or almond milk and maple syrup if needed to sweeten, and keep blending until smooth.

6 Serve the cooled flapjacks sprinkled with the remaining lemon zest and drizzled with the frosting.

Nutritional Notes

Kale and Coconut Gâteau (serves 10) Energy 595kcal/ 2470kJ; Protein 7.8g; Carbohydrate 52.2g, of which sugars 32.6g; Fat 40.2g, of which saturates 28.4g; Cholesterol 162mg; Calcium 55mg; Fibre 6.1g; Sodium 341mg.

Radish Pavlova (serves 8) Energy 262kcal/1091kJ; Protein 2.2g; Carbohydrate 25.8g, of which sugars 23g; Fat 17.4g, of which saturates 15g; Cholesterol 0mg; Calcium 13mg; Fibre 0.1g; Sodium 4mg.

Cauliflower Chocolate and Coconut Cream Layer Cake (serves 10) Energy 345kcal/1435kJ; Protein 6.1g; Carbohydrate 41.2g, of which sugars 27.1g; Fat 17.7g, of which saturates 13.6g; Cholesterol 1mg; Calcium 49mg; Fibre 3.8g; Sodium 48mg.

Red Radicchio Cake (serves 10) Energy 274kcal/1144kJ; Protein 5.8g; Carbohydrate 36.8g, of which sugars 17.3g; Fat 12.2g, of which saturates 2g; Cholesterol 69mg; Calcium 49mg; Fibre 1.5g; Sodium 169mg.

Asparagus Sesame Cake (serves 10) Energy 371kcal/ 1546kJ; Protein 6.3g; Carbohydrate 37.9g, of which sugars 19g; Fat 23.1g, of which saturates 12.7g; Cholesterol 117mg; Calcium 68mg; Fibre 3.4g; Sodium 249mg.

Carrot and Coriander Cake (makes 15 squares) Energy 205kcal/852kJ; Protein 2.9g; Carbohydrate 17.2g, of which sugars 4.9g; Fat 14.5g, of which saturates 8.2g; Cholesterol 31mg; Calcium 34mg; Fibre 1.7g; Sodium 33mg.

Godzilla Cake (serves 10) Energy 267kcal/1106kJ; Protein 2.7g; Carbohydrate 22.2g, of which sugars 16g; Fat 19.2g, of which saturates 14.3g; Cholesterol 21mg; Calcium 24mg; Fibre 3.3g; Sodium 145mg.

Tomato and Almond Cake (serves 10) Energy 554kcal/ 2303kJ; Protein 16.5g; Carbohydrate 39.7g, of which sugars 33.8g; Fat 37.6g, of which saturates 5.6g; Cholesterol 92mg; Calcium 170mg; Fibre 2.3g; Sodium 206mg.

Gidget's Gâteau (serves 8) Energy 287kcal/1197kJ; Protein 8.4g; Carbohydrate 19.7g, of which sugars 6g; Fat 20.3g, of which saturates 3.3g; Cholesterol 0mg; Calcium 76mg; Fibre 7.3g; Sodium 136mg.

Beetroot Cheesecake (serves 10) Energy 396kcal/1648kJ; Protein 7.4g; Carbohydrate 29.8g, of which sugars 14.9g; Fat 28.3g, of which saturates 15g; Cholesterol 17mg; Calcium 37mg; Fibre 4.7g; Sodium 110mg.

Fennel Pistachio Cheesecake (serves 10) Energy 404kcal/1680kJ; Protein 7.9g; Carbohydrate 28g, of which sugars 23.8g; Fat 29.7g, of which saturates 12.6g; Cholesterol 0mg; Calcium 44mg; Fibre 4.1g; Sodium 81mg.

Sunchoke Vegan Cheesecake with Hazelnuts and Orange Zest (serves 8) Energy 307kcal/1310kJ; Protein 7.8g; Carbohydrate 51.7g, of which sugars 10.5g; Fat 9.6g, of which saturates 4g; Cholesterol 15mg; Calcium 335mg; Fibre 4.2g; Sodium 58mg.

Cashew Rocket-Powdered Cheesecake (serves 10) Energy 529kcal/2197kJ; Protein 9.9g; Carbohydrate 31g, of which sugars 26.2g; Fat 41.4g, of which saturates 16.6g; Cholesterol 0mg; Calcium 81mg; Fibre 4.2g; Sodium 50mg.

Pumpkin Ginger Cheesecake (serves 10) Energy 254kcal/ 1054kJ; Protein 6.8g; Carbohydrate 16.7g, of which sugars 13.4g; Fat 18.2g, of which saturates 9.7g; Cholesterol 0mg; Calcium 208mg; Fibre 2.1g; Sodium 44mg.

Purple Prince Cheesecake (serves 10) Energy 178kcal/ 744kJ; Protein 6.9g; Carbohydrate 22.6g, of which sugars 12.6g; Fat 7.2g, of which saturates 0.9g; Cholesterol 0mg; Calcium 260mg; Fibre 3.5g; Sodium 22mg.

Maple Mushroom Cupcakes (makes 9) Energy 374kcal/ 1558kJ; Protein 10.1g; Carbohydrate 37.6g, of which sugars 17.9g; Fat 21.3g, of which saturates 8.6g; Cholesterol 79mg; Calcium 237mg; Fibre 4.9g; Sodium 389mg.

Chocolate Avocado Cauliflower Cupcakes (makes 12) Energy 206kcal/854kJ; Protein 4.3g; Carbohydrate 19.9g, of which sugars 11.3g; Fat 12.5g, of which saturates 2.4g; Cholesterol 39mg; Calcium 24mg; Fibre 2.6g; Sodium 54mg.

Lavender Spinach Cupcakes (makes 12) Energy 230kcal/ 956kJ; Protein 3.7g; Carbohydrate 17.6g, of which sugars 3.5g; Fat 16.5g, of which saturates 6.2g; Cholesterol 0mg; Calcium 69mg; Fibre 1.7g; Sodium 35mg.

Waldorf Muffins (makes 12) Energy 222kcal/929kJ; Protein 4.2g; Carbohydrate 29.2g, of which sugars 13.3g; Fat 10.7g, of which saturates 1.4g; Cholesterol 0mg; Calcium 20mg; Fibre 4.2g; Sodium 11mg.

Velvet Artichoke Hearts (makes 12) Energy 179kcal/ 745kJ; Protein 5.1g; Carbohydrate 11.9g, of which sugars 1.2g; Fat 12.8g, of which saturates 1.9g; Cholesterol 39mg; Calcium 41mg; Fibre 2g; Sodium 24mg.

Brooklyn Scones (makes 8) Energy 201kcal/840kJ; Protein 4g; Carbohydrate 28.4g, of which sugars 6.9g; Fat 8.1g, of which saturates 6.6g; Cholesterol 0mg; Calcium 25mg; Fibre 2.9g; Sodium 3mg.

Lotus Root Wrapper Cakes (makes 12) Energy 103kcal/ 430kJ; Protein 1.3g; Carbohydrate 15.9g, of which sugars 9.2g; Fat 4g, of which saturates 0.5g; Cholesterol 0mg; Calcium 27mg; Fibre 1.9g; Sodium 45mg.

Sweet Potato Fudge Blondies (makes 15) Energy 106kcal/445kJ; Protein 1.9g; Carbohydrate 14.3g, of which sugars 8.7g; Fat 4.5g, of which saturates 1g; Cholesterol 0mg; Calcium 19mg; Fibre 2.3g; Sodium 18mg.

Beetroot Rose Chocolate Brownies (makes 20) Energy 115kcal/480kJ; Protein 1g; Carbohydrate 15.3g, of which sugars 11.7g; Fat 5.9g, of which saturates 4.5g; Cholesterol 0mg; Calcium 10mg; Fibre 1g; Sodium 29mg.

Pumpkin Coffee Blondie Brownies (makes 12) Energy 134kcal/557kJ; Protein 2.7g; Carbohydrate 14g, of which sugars 6.2g; Fat 7.7g, of which saturates 1.2g; Cholesterol 0mg; Calcium 26mg; Fibre 2.2g; Sodium 2mg.

Courgette Financiers (makes 10) Energy 159kcal/658kJ; Protein 3.8g; Carbohydrate 9.1g, of which sugars 2.6g; Fat 12.1g, of which saturates 4.7g; Cholesterol 17mg; Calcium 38mg; Fibre 0.6g; Sodium 77mg.

Butternut Squash 'Donuts' (makes 10) Energy 321kcal/ 1347kJ; Protein 5.4g; Carbohydrate 42.7g, of which sugars 10g; Fat 15.5g, of which saturates 9.3g; Cholesterol 46mg; Calcium 94mg; Fibre 2.9g; Sodium 35mg.

Sweet Potato Cakes (makes 8) Energy 124kcal/520kJ; Protein 3.8g; Carbohydrate 13.7g, of which sugars 3.8g; Fat 6.4g, of which saturates 2g; Cholesterol 58mg; Calcium 37mg; Fibre 2g; Sodium 47mg.

Salted Caramel Swiss Chard Pie (serves 8) Energy 402kcal/1672kJ; Protein 4.1g; Carbohydrate 32.6g, of which sugars 11.8g; Fat 29.4g, of which saturates 18.1g; Cholesterol 102mg; Calcium 44mg; Fibre 1.5g; Sodium 290mg.

Parsnip Upside Down Tarte (serves 8) Energy 436kcal/ 1808kJ; Protein 6g; Carbohydrate 39.6g, of which sugars 21.2g; Fat 28.8g, of which saturates 15.2g; Cholesterol 116mg; Calcium 54mg; Fibre 3.3g; Sodium 232mg.

Courgette Rosette Tart (serves 12) Energy 259kcal/ 1080kJ; Protein 5.4g; Carbohydrate 25.3g, of which sugars 7.8g; Fat 15.9g, of which saturates 9.5g; Cholesterol 78mg; Calcium 54mg; Fibre 1.2g; Sodium 54mg.

Broccoli Custard Flan Slices (makes 8) Energy 370kcal/ 1538kJ; Protein 9.4g; Carbohydrate 34.3g, of which sugars 18.5g; Fat 22.3g, of which saturates 12.8g; Cholesterol 167mg; Calcium 180mg; Fibre 1.3g; Sodium 196mg.

Red Romanesco Tart (serves 12) Energy 308kcal/1281kJ; Protein 8.4g; Carbohydrate 13.3g, of which sugars 12.5g; Fat 25g, of which saturates 12.7g; Cholesterol 19mg; Calcium 68mg; Fibre 1.9g; Sodium 18mg.

Fiddlehead Fern Galette Tart (serves 8) Energy 276kcal/ 1153kJ; Protein 3.9g; Carbohydrate 31.6g, of which sugars 11.8g; Fat 15.6g, of which saturates 4.9g; Cholesterol 0mg; Calcium 129mg; Fibre 2.6g; Sodium 193mg.

Brussels Hazelnut Frangipane Tart (serves 10) Energy 359kcal/1488kJ; Protein 5.9g; Carbohydrate 11.8g, of which sugars 5.5g; Fat 31.8g, of which saturates 10g; Cholesterol 35mg; Calcium 57mg; Fibre 4.6g; Sodium 104mg.

Maple Lemon Veggie Slab Pie (serves 8) Energy 325kcal/ 1359kJ; Protein 5.4g; Carbohydrate 38.5g, of which sugars 12.1g; Fat 17.6g, of which saturates 10.3g; Cholesterol 94mg; Calcium 96mg; Fibre 4g; Sodium 144mg.

Corn, Sage and Apricot Cookies (makes 25) Energy 69kcal/288kJ; Protein 1.4g; Carbohydrate 8.7g, of which sugars 3.4g; Fat 3.4g, of which saturates 1.8g; Cholesterol 25mg; Calcium 13mg; Fibre 0.5g; Sodium 54mg.

Kale Matcha Cookies (makes 20) Energy 106kcal/442kJ; Protein 1.6g; Carbohydrate 12.9g, of which sugars 6.7g; Fat 5.7g, of which saturates 3.2g; Cholesterol 12mg; Calcium 14mg; Fibre 1.3g; Sodium 44mg.

Pumpkin Cookies (makes 12) Energy 142kcal/596kJ; Protein 4g; Carbohydrate 11.6g, of which sugars 0.6g; Fat 8.7g, of which saturates 2.8g; Cholesterol 0mg; Calcium 14mg; Fibre 2.4g; Sodium 22mg.

Spinach Macarons (makes 20) Energy 90kcal/375kJ; Protein 2.2g; Carbohydrate 9.6g, of which sugars 9.3g; Fat 5g, of which saturates 0.8g; Cholesterol 1mg; Calcium 44mg; Fibre 0.5g; Sodium 31mg.

Cakey Cauli Cookies (makes 12) Energy 135kcal/560kJ; Protein 2.7g; Carbohydrate 15.2g, of which sugars 5.9g; Fat 7.5g, of which saturates 5.8g; Cholesterol 19mg; Calcium 24mg; Fibre 2.8g; Sodium 21mg.

Nettle Biscotti with Bitters (makes 10) Energy 243kcal/ 1016kJ; Protein 6.1g; Carbohydrate 29.7g, of which sugars 10.1g; Fat 11.9g, of which saturates 1.2g; Cholesterol 46mg; Calcium 71mg; Fibre 0.3g; Sodium 56mg.

Carrot Linzer Cookies (makes 25) Energy 161kcal/670kJ; Protein 2.6g; Carbohydrate 14.6g, of which sugars 6.4g; Fat 10.7g, of which saturates 4.6g; Cholesterol 25mg; Calcium 33mg; Fibre 0.7g; Sodium 60mg.

Mizuna Macaroons (makes 12) Energy 82kcal/341kJ; Protein 0.7g; Carbohydrate 7.2g, of which sugars 6.7g; Fat 5.8g, of which saturates 4.8g; Cholesterol 0mg; Calcium 11mg; Fibre 1.7g; Sodium 11mg.

Parsnip, Swede and Hazelnut Flapjacks (makes 12) Energy 256kcal/1073kJ; Protein 4.4g; Carbohydrate 39.5g, of which sugars 16.1g; Fat 9.9g, of which saturates 5g; Cholesterol 0mg; Calcium 39mg; Fibre 4.1g; Sodium 24mg.

Index

COOK'S NOTES:

Bracketed terms are intended for American readers. For all recipes, quantities are given in both metric and imperial measures and, where appropriate, in standard US cups and spoons. Follow one set of measures, but not a mixture, because they are not interchangeable. Standard spoon and cup measures are level. 1 tsp = 5ml, 1 tbsp = 15ml, 1 cup = 250ml/8fl oz. Australian standard tablespoons are 20ml. Australian readers can use 3 tsp in place of 1 tbsp for measuring small quantities. American pints are 16fl oz/2 cups. American readers should use 20fl oz/2.5 cups in place of 1 pint when measuring liquids.

Electric oven temperatures in this book are for conventional ovens. When using a fan oven, the temperature will probably need to be reduced by about 10–20°C/20–40°F. Since ovens vary, check with your manufacturer's instruction book for guidance.

The nutritional analysis given for each recipe is calculated per portion (i.e. serving or item), unless otherwise stated. If the recipe gives a range, such as Serves 4–6, then the nutritional analysis will be for the smaller portion size, i.e. 6 servings. The analysis does not include optional ingredients.

This edition is published by Lorenz Books
an imprint of Anness Publishing Ltd
www.annesspublishing.com
info@anness.com
twitter: @AnnessLorenzBks

© Anness Publishing Ltd 2018

Publisher: Joanna Lorenz
Recipe contributor: Liz O'Keefe
Photography and prop styling: Nicki Dowey
Food stylist: Liz O'Keefe
Editorial: Sarah Lumby, Helen Sudell
Nutritionist: Clare Emery
Designer: Adelle Mahoney

With thanks to William Shaw for additional images and Shutterstock for the pictures on 44 and 106.

Publishers' note: the advice and information in this book are believed to be accurate and true at the time of going to press; neither the author nor the publishers can accept any legal responsibility or liability for any errors or omissions that may have been made nor for any inaccuracies nor for any loss, harm or injury that comes about from following instructions or advice in this book. It is advisable to consult a qualified medical professional before undertaking a dietary regime.

ABOUT THE AUTHOR:

Ysanne Spevack was born and raised in London before travelling to Los Angeles in 2004, where she lived for a decade before moving to New York, where she now divides her time with London. In California, she managed organic estates and orchards in Malibu and Topanga. In New York, her food took her in other directions, cooking for private clients. Her first book, *The Organic Cookbook*, also published by Lorenz Books, sells around the world, and her trove of other books includes *The Ranch Cookbook* for Rizzoli; *Fresh & Wild: A Real Food Adventure* for HarperCollins; and *The Real Taste of Japan*. Her recent book, *The No-Sugar Desserts and Baking Book*, is a glorious journey into baking without refined sugar. She has written for the Los Angeles Times Food Section, the Observer Food Monthly, and leading magazines and newspapers internationally. From edible gardens to her travelling kitchen, Ysanne creates recipes that deliver the flavours you crave, with a deep understanding of the ingredients at the root of each dish, including their origins and therapeutic qualities. Herbs, flowers, salts and spices magically add warmth, fragrance, minerals and heat. Using this broad knowledge, Ysanne has created Yntegrity, a series of immersive experiences for the senses, including taste, smell, vision, audition, and touch. For more information about go to TasteColors.com and Yntegrity.com.

Author's dedication:

And finally, a note for everyone, adults and children alike, to remember that vegetables can never, ever be used in cakes, it's impossible! And yet, here it is – a book of recipes for undeniably delicious vegetable cakes, and so, well.. it seems anything is possible! Therefore, let's all believe six impossible things before breakfast every day, exactly as the Queen herself recommends. I particularly want to suggest some of my favourite children do this, and that would have to include Aasha, Ellie, Michael, Phoebe, Frida, Felix, Freddie, Ingrid, Ulysses, Garnet, Oskar, Tommy Jr, Daisy and baby Iris. You are my inspiration!